THE BOOK ON
Tax Strategies for the

SAVVY
REAL ESTATE
INVESTOR

THE BOOK ON
Tax Strategies for the
SAVVY
REAL ESTATE
INVESTOR

Powerful techniques anyone can use
to deduct more, invest smarter, and
pay far less to the IRS!

By Amanda Han and Matthew MacFarland

BiggerPockets
PUBLISHING

This publication is designed to provide general information regarding the subject matter covered. It is not intended to serve as legal, tax, or other financial advice related to individual situations. Because each individual's legal, tax, and financial situation are different, specific advice should be tailored to their particular circumstances. For this reason, you are advised to consult with your own attorney, CPA, and/or other advisor regarding your specific situation.

The information and all accompanying material are for your use and convenience only. We have taken reasonable precautions in the preparation of this material and believe that the information presented in this material is accurate as of the date it was written. However, we will assume no responsibility for any errors or omissions. We specifically disclaim any liability resulting from the use or application of the information contained in this book.

To ensure compliance with requirements imposed by the IRS, we inform you that any US federal tax advice contained in this communication (including any attachments) is not intended or written to be used, and it cannot be used for the purpose of (i) avoiding penalties under the Internal Revenue Code or (ii) promoting, marketing, or recommending to another party any transaction or matter addressed herein. Always seek advice based on your particular circumstances from an independent advisor.

Any trademarks, service marks, product names, and named features are assumed to be the property of their respective owners and are used only for reference. No endorsement is implied when we use one of these terms.

Any disclosure, copying, or distribution of this material, or the taking of any action based on it, is strictly prohibited.

The Book on Tax Strategies for the Savvy Real Estate Investor
Amanda Han and Matthew MacFarland

Published by BiggerPockets Publishing, LLC, Denver, CO
Copyright © 2016 by Tax Strategies Institute, LLC. All Rights Reserved.

Publisher's Cataloging-in-Publication
(Provided by Quality Books, Inc.)

    Han, Amanda, author.
      The book on tax strategies for the savvy real estate
    investor : powerful techniques anyone can use to deduct
    more, invest smarter, and pay far less to the IRS! / by
    Amanda Han and Matthew MacFarland.
      pages cm
      ISBN 978-0-9907117-6-6
      ISBN 978-0-9907117-4-2

      1. Real estate investment--Taxation--Law and
    legislation--United States--Popular works. 2. Real
    property and taxation--United States--Popular works.
    3. Tax planning--United States--Popular works. 4. Law for
    laypersons.   I. MacFarland, Matthew, author.
    II. Title.

    KF6540.H36 2016   343.7305'46
                    QBI16-900057

Printed in the United States of America
10 9 8 7 6 5 4 3

Dedication

This book is dedicated to real estate investors everywhere: May this book bring you the power & knowledge needed to keep more of your hard earned money every year.

Contents

IRS PITFALLS 117

CONCLUSION 161

In America, there are two tax systems: one for the informed and one for the uninformed. Both are legal.

– Judge Billings Learned Hand

Message from the Authors

This is not a rags-to-riches real estate story. We were not poor growing up, and we did not become the next Donald Trump.

Real estate is not our passion. Let us say that again—real estate is not our passion. So if you have picked up this book to learn the ins and outs of how to invest in real estate, this book may not be what you are looking for. This is just a story by two accountants who want to share their personal experiences with tax strategies for real estate investors

Money, on the other hand, is our passion. Helping people keep more of their hard-earned income is definitely our passion. Although this book is about real estate, it just may be a little different from the usual real estate books you have read. This book explains why we invested in real estate, how we use it to save on taxes, and how you can do the same.

Actually, we never cared too much about our own taxes. Shocking to hear from two certified public accountants (CPAs) who specialize in taxes, right? In fact, not only did we not pay attention to our own taxes, but we had even less knowledge about money, investing, and wealth building. Working for over half a decade at one of the largest and most prestigious accounting firms in the world, we—along with several of our colleagues—had no knowledge of these "things"—the very "things" people paid us a lot of money to advise them on. It took several years but we did finally learn how to use the tax code to save on taxes for ourselves and how to best build our own wealth.

We wrote this book to share with you the inside secrets that may help you keep more of your hard-earned money. These are secrets your CPA may not have told you or may never tell you, such as the most common and costly tax mistakes you may be making as a real estate investor and why your CPA may be costing you more money than you think. We also wanted to expose some of the common and costly tax myths we hear about year after year.

This book is not about how to invest in real estate. It is about how to use real estate to shelter your taxes and accelerate your wealth building. If you are an experienced investor, you will learn about tax strategies designed especially to help investors like you keep more of your bottom line. And if you are new to real estate investing, even better! These strategies will help you plan your future so you don't make the tax mistakes many others do.

Through stories based on those of actual clients with various types of real estate businesses, from rental to wholesale to fix and flip, our goal is to share the strategies we believe can help you keep more of your money from Uncle Sam.

Introduction

What You <u>Will Not</u> Find in This Book

What you will not find in this book are tax code citations, regulations, or references to court cases. If you want those, you can get a copy of the Internal Revenue Service (IRS) tax code and the thousands of pages of its related regulations. Our goal was to write a tax strategy book that would not put you to sleep.

When we teach tax classes for investors all over the United States, the most common and consistent feedback we receive is that we make our presentations easy for the average investor to understand. To break away from the usual boring tax book, we set out to write a tax book in plain English instead of in "tax code."

What You <u>Will</u> Find in This Book

In this book, you will learn about everyday investors who make small changes that have a dramatic impact on their taxes and finances. You will hear real stories of clients we have worked with and the actions they have taken to supercharge their wealth building.

Now let us warn you, it is not all pretty. You will laugh, you will sigh, and you may even cry at some of the painful mistakes that cost people lots and lots of money. Why? Because these are real-life stories, and real life is not always magic fairy dust and happy endings. But within every story lies a lesson or strategy that may help you reduce your tax burden and keep more of your money.

Amanda: Growing Up as the Landlord's Grandchild

Amanda's grandparents emigrated from Taiwan to the United States in the 1970s. They settled in Las Vegas and bought some land and rental properties—and by "some," we mean roughly 40 condo units. Amanda and her parents arrived in the United States a few years later, and boy, did Amanda have fun living there! At that point, Amanda was in the second grade, and she started school in the middle of December, which was great. Between Santa Claus, reindeer, and candy canes, Amanda's first two weeks of school were heavenly.

The other thing Amanda loved about her new home in the United States was that she was living with a lot of people. To say it was a large family in a small space would be an understatement. In their single three-bedroom condo resided Amanda, her mom and dad, her grandparents, and her uncle and cousin. For Amanda, living there was great. One of her favorite things she and her cousin did while growing up was help clean the rental units after tenants moved out.

Amanda would always be so excited when tenants moved out, because she knew that soon, she would get to sweep the floors and paint the walls. She thought growing up in the condo complex was wonderful. There was something special about being "the landlord's grandkid." There was always something to do, and everyone was nicer to her—or at least it seemed that way.

But being the landlord's grandkid was not all fun and games; Amanda also learned some things about real estate investing that were not so pleasant. For example, sometimes you can have bad tenants—ones who don't pay and then move out in the dark of night, taking everything with them. And sometimes you get the complainers—people who call you every other day asking you to fix one thing or the next.

So for these reasons, Amanda never thought she would invest in real estate herself when she grew up. It was more of a headache than it was worth. Not until many years later, when Amanda was working as a CPA in corporate America, did she finally learn that real estate is one of the best-kept secrets to wealth building.

Matt: Growing Up as the Doctor's Child

Matt also grew up in a large family. Matt's parents divorced when he was young, so he and his brother were used to splitting time between their parents and stepparents. Matt's stepfather was a pediatrician, and his mom worked both morning and night shifts as a nurse so she could spend more time with the boys.

Matt recalls that when he was growing up, people would always talk about how wonderful it would be if Matt became a doctor like his stepfather Jerry. Matt was great with little kids, and he excelled in math and science at school. It seemed like a great plan for him to get into the medical field—that is, until he and his family learned of his fear of blood and needles.

Growing up with parents and stepparents who all worked full-time as professionals, Matt was brought up to be conservative with his finances. His parents taught him the value of a dollar and the importance of saving money for a rainy day. Matt recalls having very little exposure to ideas of how to invest and grow money. The only recollection he has from his childhood of what an investment property could do for you is actually pretty horrific.

You see, in the '70s and '80s, the tax code was somewhat different from how it is today. Some of the loopholes still exist, just in a different form. Back then, many doctors would invest in certain real estate partnerships in hopes of taking large tax deductions and striking it rich at the same time. Financial regulations were much more lax, and many investors lost significant amounts of money in these partnership investments that went very bad very quickly.

As you may have guessed, Matt's stepfather was one such doctor. After investing several years' worth of hard-earned money in these real estate partnership deals only to lose a large portion of it, his stepfather was done with real estate forever. Even though Matt was too young at that time to really understand the investment side of things, he did understand that his family had lost a good chunk of money to "bad real estate." In Matt's mind, real estate was something very risky that he should stay far away from. It would take several more years to change Matt's perspective on real estate. However, he would one day realize all the benefits of being a real estate investor with the help of a little-known book.

Amanda and Matt: The Traditional Route

Over the next several years after graduating from high school, we both did exactly what our parents taught us to do: go to school, get good grades, and get good jobs.

We were both always great with numbers and naturally excelled in college in business and accounting. After graduation, we were ecstatic when we received offers to work as tax advisors at one of the largest international accounting firms in the world. And by happenstance, we were both assigned to the real estate specialty group. So, as you may have guessed, we had arrived! We had fulfilled our parents' wishes to go to college and get a good job.

Over the next few years, we both obtained our CPA licenses and dated in secrecy while working at the same firm. Several years later, we got married and made a home together.

What You Don't Know Can Hurt You

Ever hear the phrase "What you don't know can hurt you"? Well, that basically described our situation. You see, we were stuck in the rat race. Together, we were making a little over $200,000 a year at our jobs. We put a good chunk of our income into our 401(k)s each year, and money was never an issue for us. But after about two years of marriage, we realized that we hadn't accumulated as much money as we thought we should have, based on our earnings. So of course, as accountants, we took the time to look at our numbers, and what we found was shocking.

After analyzing our finances, we realized that we were losing roughly $50,000 per year to Uncle Sam in federal income taxes. In addition, we were paying roughly $16,000 each year in state income taxes. The payroll taxes withheld from our paychecks each year totaled about $14,000. And last but not least, the property taxes on our modest three-bedroom home were roughly $3,000 each year. Adding all this up, we realized we were paying close to $90,000 in taxes each year. Almost one-half of our annual income was being lost to taxes before we even spent a dime of it. Plus, from household items to groceries, even more of our money was lost to sales taxes.

This finding surprised both of us. We had not realized that so much of our money was being lost to taxes. If you think about it, one of us was working mainly to pay our taxes, right? We found out early in my career that

6

there is a day called Tax Freedom Day, and contrary to popular belief, it is not the day your taxes are due. Tax Freedom Day generally occurs sometime in April, and it is the day when the nation as a whole has theoretically earned enough income to pay its taxes for the year. For example, if Tax Freedom Day were April 30th, then all the money you had earned from January 1st to April 30th would be paid toward taxes. Then, May 1st would be the first day you got to keep your earnings free from taxes (see Appendix A for details).

We were distraught after learning about our massive tax bill and shocked to see the real reason we had been slow to build our wealth. Now, given that we are two CPAs who specialize in the tax field, you will find what we did next shocking!

What Do Most Americans Do About Taxes?

What we did next was nothing. That's right! After finding out that we lose roughly 50% of our earnings each year to taxes, we did nothing! Sure, we moaned and groaned about it for a few days and complained about how unfair the U.S. tax system is, but we did absolutely nothing to change anything.

Why, you may ask? Well, for the same reason most Americans ignore their taxes. April is the one time each year that we as Americans collectively complain about taxes and our taxation system. Then, life happens, and we forget all about our tax gripes and move on with our daily lives until the next tax season.

We were no different. After working twelve- to fourteen-hour days to resolve financial and tax issues for our clients, the last thing we wanted to do at the end of our busy day was look over our own finances. Funny, right? It's just like how you hear that doctors make the worst patients. I guess in our situation, CPAs make the worst taxpayers. Besides, we were also busy with other stuff, such as making improvements to our new house and spending time with family and friends. Heck, we were even starting to have conversations about starting a family sometime soon.

The Book That Opened the Door to a Whole New Way of Looking at Wealth Building

So life went on as before—no more complaints about taxes or our finances. It was a problem we both knew we had but were almost afraid to address.

It wasn't until we read the book *Rich Dad Poor Dad* by Robert T. Kiyosaki that we started to look at our personal wealth building through a different set of eyes. Matt actually read the book first, which piqued his interest and curiosity about how this could help improve our situation. In the beginning, we were not on the same page when Matt announced that we should buy one or two rental properties to begin building our wealth.

"Have you thought about the headaches of rental real estate?" Amanda asked. "Are you prepared to deal with crazy tenants who don't pay or having to get out of bed in the middle of the night to unclog toilets? I bet not. Trust me, we should definitely not buy rental real estate. It requires a ton of work and a ton of time, time that we don't have. I grew up in my grandparents' condo rentals, remember? Trust me, I know all about the nightmares of real estate investing, and that is definitely not what we want to do."

"I think you are looking at this the wrong way," Matt responded. "I think we need to look at this from a wealth-building and tax perspective. Tell me, who are your highest-income clients, and what do they do?"

Amanda thought about it for a brief moment, and a name immediately popped into her head: Jim Wellington. Jim used to be an engineer by trade. Once he and his wife had their first baby, they bought their first rental property. That property was intended to generate college money for their baby. Then Jim had a few more kids and bought more rentals, each intended as a tool to pay for the kids' college tuition. Over the years, he traded his rentals up and got into apartment investing. Today, he owns most of the apartments for rent in the Westwood, California area. In fact, he liked it when Amanda once told him they should rename Westwood Wellington. The truth was, Jim did not deal directly with any of his tenants. He had property managers who did all that for him. He worked very little and was able to travel and enjoy time with his family and children.

Amanda also knew that Jim made roughly $500,000 a year in rental income, on which he paid little to no taxes, thanks to depreciation, legal entity structures, and various other tax strategies he used each year.

"So you mean to tell me that Jim, one of your clients, works very few hours, makes roughly $500,000 per year on his rentals, and pays zero taxes. Is that right?" Matt asked.

The answer had been right in front of us the whole time. Day in and day out, we worked with clients who had similar situations. Looking back on all our truly successful clients, most were either real estate investors or business owners, and much of the time, they were both. There was no reason we shouldn't follow that same path: make money, invest money, and minimize our taxes.

Taking the First Step into the Unknown

We have to admit, buying our first rental property was one of the scariest things we had ever done. It is probably the biggest investment decision we have ever made together, and we were both scared to death. But it got better each time. The more properties we looked at, negotiated, and purchased, the better and easier the process became for us.

What also helped us tremendously was taking real estate investing classes. We tried to attend as many classes as we could to learn from other investors. Another great resource was our local real estate investment clubs and associations. It was always great to learn what other investors were doing and to pick their brains on what works well and what doesn't in the investing business.

As we were growing our real estate investments, we were also building a reputation for ourselves. As soon as someone found out we were real estate investors, they would ask us all sorts of questions like "What type of legal entity should we form?" and "Can I deduct the cost of my classes?" and "What do I need to do to write off my car?" and so on, and so on.

It wasn't long before we realized that there was a huge need within the community for some real estate–savvy tax advice. I guess we were never aware that a whole community existed that didn't comprise people like Jim Wellington, just your average real estate investors who were trying to make life better for their families.

The solution soon became clear to us. We would fill that void. We would take the financial and tax strategies we knew from our job, which was designed to help minimize taxes for the super wealthy, and tailor them to the needs of the average investor, like the new friends we had met at various real estate training classes and our local real estate investment clubs. These were investors just like the two of us. The more we worked with these investor communities, the more we became aware of the problems they faced.

One of the problems we see time and time again is that most CPAs work with a large variety of clients rather than specializing in a particular industry. What we learned when we started working with real estate investors is that many of them have been working with the wrong advisors, ones who did not specialize in real estate. And as a result, we saw common mistakes and heard many myths that were costing people tons of money.

We were on a mission to help the real estate community understand the tax strategies and loopholes that were available to them as investors. However, as you can imagine, there just aren't enough hours in the day for us to do that for everyone. With hundreds of thousands of real estate investors all across the country, the two of us could not possibly share our strategies with everyone in person. We are not a large CPA firm, nor do we have hundreds of people working for us. Even though we work with clients all over the United States, we are small enough that we know all our clients intimately. Because the majority of our clients have real estate investments, we spend a large percentage of our time keeping ourselves up-to-date on real estate–related issues and strategies.

Why Most Tax Strategy Books Do Not Help Readers

As an investor, you do not need to understand everything there is to know about taxes. You do not need to read the tax code, and you do not need to learn to decipher all the court cases and the related regulations.

As CPAs, we have read dozens of tax strategy books for business and real estate. Although many books are available on how to save on taxes, most readers find these books of little help.

A major reason for this is that the majority of the tax books are written with too many technical terms. Some are just a regurgitation of the IRS tax code. What we have found is that these tax strategy books spend a lot of time referencing code sections that do not make much sense to the average American reader, and very often, there are not enough examples given of how the strategies are used and how the reader can take action.

The remainder of this book is filled with stories, real-life stories about average investors, just like you and like us. You will read success stories of people who used simple strategies to dramatically slash their tax bill. You will hear stories of how a small mistake can cost investors a large amount of their hard-earned money. You will also learn about some of the most commonly heard myths and what the truth behind them really is. More importantly, there will be stories that reveal how people can supercharge their wealth building when empowered with the right information and knowledge. Our hope is that from these stories, you will get ideas and strategies you can use to reduce your taxes and create a better financial future for yourself.

DEDUCTIONS

What Can You Really Deduct?

The hardest thing in the world to understand is the income tax.

— Albert Einstein

If you feel taxes are complicated, you are in good company. The founder of the theory of relativity (whose name is synonymous with genius) was so confounded by his income tax forms that after reading through them, he gave up in despair and hired a tax specialist to help file his taxes.

Have you ever tried to read the tax code and its regulations? It has a language all its own. Nothing seems to be in plain English. With pages and pages of lengthy and unnecessarily vague sentences and references to other code sections, it is no wonder that even the smartest minds in history have been frustrated by our tax code.

In addition to the complexity of the subject matter, the U.S. tax code is lengthy. It is estimated by CNN to be roughly 73,954 pages long (and growing). This is just the official tax code itself. Then there are thousands and thousands of pages of Treasury Regulations that are the official and temporary interpretations of the Internal Revenue Code. Yes, that is right—the code is so confusing that we actually have thousands and thousands of pages just to interpret what the code actually means. Isn't that ludicrous?

Now, if that were the end of the story, it may not be too bad. But the other issue is that the tax code is an ever-changing and ever-growing monster. In fact, since 2001, there have been approximately 4,680 changes made to the tax code. This is an average of one change per day, and when the tax code changes, so do the thousands of pages of treasury regulations that explain the code. It takes an army of tax professionals to help Americans navigate all the complexities. In fact, tax preparation takes up approximately 6.1 billion hours in the United States each and every year. No wonder the average American doesn't understand how taxes affect their bottom line.

So why do so many Americans end up overpaying their taxes each year? Well, the biggest reason is that most people just don't understand what they can deduct as legitimate write-offs on their tax returns.

What You Might Be Missing on Your Tax Returns

Real Life: Our client Nancy told us when we first started preparing her returns that she had zero car and travel expenses related to her rental properties, because all her rentals were out of state, and she never drove to visit any of them. She was purely a passive investor, and in fact, she never even saw the properties before purchasing them. She bought them from a turnkey company that sold them to her after they had been fully fixed up and with tenants already in place, so Nancy was sure she did not have any car-related expenses to write off on her taxes.

What Nancy did not know was that as a real estate investor, you are not limited to writing off car expenses only for visits to your rental property. There are all sorts of other times when you can take advantage of car or other legitimate business write-offs.

Nancy was always actively looking for properties to invest in. Once she had a few rental properties under her belt, she began look-ing locally for her next rental property. Her mileage and car expenses while driving around to scope out neighborhoods and attend open houses may be tax deductible. Nancy liked to keep her pulse on the local market, and from time to time, she would even take a local real estate agent out to lunch to try to get some pocket listings before they hit the market. What Nancy didn't know was that the cost of lunch with these real estate agents, as well as her related driving expenses, was tax deductible.

Even though Nancy was fairly new to real estate, she was de-termined to learn everything she could to supercharge her investing *potential. She joined several local real estate clubs and associations to network with other investors so that she could find partners to work with and better ways of getting cash for new deals. Not only was the mileage to her local club meetings tax deductible, but so were her club membership dues. In fact, Nancy regularly attended two to three real estate club meetings each month, none of which she took tax write-offs for. On an annual basis, her travel costs around town for her meetings and property hunting resulted in close to $900 in tax deductions. Add that to the membership costs and meals that she would sometimes have after these investor meetings, and the total tax deductions on these expenses ended up close to $1,800 in just one year.*

As real estate investors, we are all very good at writing off real estate–specific items, such as mortgage interest, insurance premiums, property taxes, management fees, and repairs and maintenance. However, what most investors forget to write off are the overhead expenses they may incur because of their rental property.

For example, most real estate investors will have some sort of marketing expenses, such as from posting rentals in the newspaper or online or printing out flyers to post around the neighborhood. These marketing expenses are tax-deductible write-offs as well.

Another commonly missed overhead expense is car and travel deductions. For investors with local rentals, it is common to drive to the property to do some light repairs, pick up rent checks, and the like. Maybe you are someone who likes to drive a little out of the way to creep by your rental with your headlights turned off, just to make sure the tenants are not burning the house down (yes, we admit we have done this ourselves in dire situations). The miles you drive to visit your rental properties are tax deductible, too, so be sure to keep track of them.

Making it a Habit

The number one reason people often miss out on taking these overhead real estate expenses as deductions on their tax return is that they don't know that they can. This is something that can easily be learned. In fact, by reading this book, you are learning a ton about which items can be tax deductible. To be truly successful in keeping every penny of your hard-earned money, make sure to make taxes a part of your everyday life.

We are not talking about walking around thinking "taxes, taxes, taxes" all day long. (Yes, it's possible that we as CPAs do that, but we don't expect everyone else to do it, too.) We are talking about making tax planning part of your system and thought process. For example, before you purchase that new iPad, think about some ways you could write it off as an expense related to your real estate business. Or if you are planning a trip to Florida next summer, what are some ways you could write off a large part of that trip as a business expense?

Learning to think creatively and proactively about ways to minimize your taxes and how this applies to day-to-day things will help you keep more of your profit in your pocket rather than handing it over to the IRS. We know that some of you may think what we have described is the job of your CPA or tax preparer, but that would be as incorrect as saying that your doctor takes care of your body. The reality is that you are the person who takes care of your body. You do so by choosing what you eat, what you drink, how much you sleep, and how much you exercise. Your doctor simply guides you in the right direction to be as healthy as possible and helps cure illnesses when necessary.

Similarly, on the financial and tax side, it is important to understand that you are in control of your tax bill. Although your CPA can help you maximize your deductions, it is equally important that you understand the basics of what each decision means to your financial state of health. Your CPA can give you advice and suggest possible routes to take with your business, but it is up to you as the taxpayer to implement the suggestions, educate yourself, and think of things from a tax-planning perspective. By taking the time to read this book and understand some of the strategies and commonly missed tax write-offs, you have taken the first step to keeping more of your bottom line.

You may be shocked to hear that a large percentage of people still choose to not claim these legitimate business expenses even after learning that they can write them off. We bet that even after reading our story about Nancy, you still may not write off these car, club, or meal expenses. Why is that? Well, the possibilities and excuses are infinite, but here are two main reasons.

Number one: You may be too lazy to track the expenses. After all, who wants to keep track of miles that you drive when looking for properties or going to real estate meetings, especially if you are just driving locally? Ten miles here and there may not seem significant at all. Most of the time, we are rushing from one place to the next anyway, and we may forget to clock our miles. Ten miles turns into one hundred very quickly. If mileage tracking does not become a habit, chances are good that we won't even think about writing off our miles until tax time, when our tax advisors ask about such expenses, only to get a blank stare from us: "Miles? I have no idea."

Number two: Who doesn't hate those thin, tiny restaurant receipts that get crumbled and lost so easily? They accumulate in our wallets and purses and start taking over our cars and desks. A question in the minds of many people is this: Do we really need to keep receipts? Unfortunately, the unpopular answer is yes, you do need to keep most receipts.

So how do we overcome these hurdles? Well, the best way is to create systems for your real estate business to automate and streamline as much as possible. With respect to mileage and receipts, the two largest sources of complaints we hear from lazy investors, check out the following tips.

Mileage

If your travel is fairly consistent, you can actually keep detailed records for a period of time and then apply that to the entire year. In Nancy's example, if she drives to the same two or three local real estate club meetings each month, she should be able to find out the distance from her home office to the meeting location once and then multiply that number by the number of such meetings she attended to get her total miles driven for real estate meetings for the entire year. In this case, you only have to do one month of work, and then you're scot-free for the remaining eleven, unless things drastically change, of course. If you move or cancel a membership, then you may need to recalculate.

Receipts

With respect to receipts, your cell phone can be your best friend. Who doesn't have a cell phone with a camera these days? I mean, even our 85-year-old grandma can be seen taking pictures of her great-grandkids everywhere with her cell phone. A great tip is to take a picture of those meal or store receipts with your cell phone right when you get them. Then, once a month, you can upload those photos to a folder on your computer. That way, if you are ever audited, you will be able to just go back to that folder to get an electronic copy of any receipt for documentation support. Once a picture has been taken of a receipt, you can shred that actual receipt and never have to look for it again. Yes, a scanned copy of the receipt is valid for IRS purposes!

BONUS TIP: You should also keep notes about the business purpose of the expense. For example, if it was a business meal, you should keep track of whom you met with and what you discussed.

If we want to maximize our tax write-offs, the first thing we must master is making taxes part of our daily lives, to always be conscious of when something could be a tax write-off. Making it second nature could help increase your deductions and save taxes in the end. So don't focus only on the mortgage, taxes, and repair expenses for your real estate investments. Next time you check out a property, meet with an investor, or attend a local real estate investor association meeting, be sure to keep taxes in the back of your mind and maximize your write-offs as you go. Don't forget, the money you paid for this book should be a tax deduction as well, so take a picture of that payment receipt before you forget about it.

What Does All This Mean?

One of the easiest ways for us as investors to minimize our tax burden is to simply capture and claim all the legitimate expenses we are entitled to. Given that some of the overhead expenses are the most commonly forgotten write-offs for investors, a good habit to get into is making tax savings part of your daily routine. This way, you maximize the possibility of a tax deduction.

To save time and avoid missed deductions, look at ways to create systems that work for you to help you systemize and automate your receipt and mileage tracking. Don't forget that real estate deductions do not have to relate to a specific property. If the expense helps you in your real estate investing, you can likely take it as a tax deduction.

When in doubt, be sure to consult with your tax advisor so they can help you strategize on what items can be potential tax deductions.

Dare to Deduct That?

Don't think outside the box. Think like there is no box.

— Unknown

What can I deduct? This is the most common question we get as CPAs— and it is hard to answer. In fact, it is almost impossible to answer, and here is why: *anything* can be tax deductible. Whether you can write something off or not depends on your personal and business situation.

One of the most frequent complaints we hear from investors is that they dread tax time. Now you may think that people dread meeting with their CPAs because CPAs can be boring or geeky, or that tax time is so dreadful because there is so much work to be done. But these are not actually the main reasons people dread tax time. In reality, one of the most common reasons is the unknown. Let's face it, most people just do not understand what they can deduct. For many, there is always the nagging question of "What am I missing out on?" The tax code is extremely complex and should be read only by those needing to cure an extreme case of insomnia—you do not need to memorize the code to minimize your taxes as an investor! From the hundreds and hundreds of pages of tax and legal jargon, the main thing the average taxpayer needs to understand is the definition of "business expenses." This is so important because, for the most part, personal expenses generally are not deductible, whereas business expenses are tax deductible.

For example, if you bought a laptop that you use primarily for personal reasons like surfing the Web, watching Netflix, or shopping online, you would not get a tax deduction for it. On the other hand, if you bought a laptop that you use primarily for your real estate business to manage properties, deals, and bookkeeping, then the cost of that laptop may be tax deductible. Depending on your tax rate, you could save up to 50% or more in income taxes with that laptop you bought. The same goes for all sorts of other items, such as the following examples:

Purse = Nondeductible	Work Briefcase = Deductible
Personal Phone = Nondeductible	Business Phone = Deductible
Personal Meal = Nondeductible	Business Meal = Deductible
Personal Travel = Nondeductible	Business Travel = Deductible
Personal Car = Nondeductible	Business Car = Deductible

What is a Business Deduction?

So what exactly is a business deduction? The IRS has only two criteria it considers to determine whether a deduction is business related:

Number one: To be a legitimate business deduction, the expense must be ordinary in the course of your business. In other words, is this an expense that occurs commonly in your business? In the real estate world, for example, having banners and signs as expenses is common. Whether you are a landlord, real estate agent, or flipper, banners and signs are a common way of advertising your properties. Therefore, these may represent a deductible expense for your properties.

Number two: To be a legitimate business deduction, the expense must be necessary in the course of your business. In other words, this is an expense that you must incur to create profit as a real estate investor. A common necessary expense in the real estate world would be homeowners association (HOA) fees. This expense is necessary, because if you didn't pay the fees, you could be subject to hefty fines and penalties from your HOA board. Therefore, these payments are legitimate business deductions. As long as an expense is both ordinary and necessary to your real estate business, you can generally take it as a tax deduction.

Now, these two examples—banners/signs and HOA fees—are clearly business expenses. They are expenses that most, if not all, real estate investors encounter at some point. But what are some other, less common expenses we might see?

Real Life: *Karen is a longtime real estate investor. She purchased her first rental property when she was in her early twenties and barely out of college. Unlike most people in the real estate business, Karen did not have a master plan to become a real estate guru. In fact, we call her the "accidental real estate investor," because she essentially stumbled into real estate investing unintentionally.*

Karen was a business consultant for Fortune 500 companies. Although most consultants rotate from client to client every few weeks, Karen usually took two to three years to complete a consulting project. Her employer would pay for her to stay in hotels near her clients, but Karen disliked living in a hotel room. The small living quarters were bad enough, but she was also a neat freak and hated the idea of sleeping in a bed that hundreds of strangers had used before her.

So, rather than having her employer pay for her hotel stay, Karen opted for a living stipend and used that money to buy a small condo close to her current consulting project. Then, when she was finished with the consulting job, she would find a new tenant to move into her condo, and she would move on to her next project in a different city. Over the years, she managed to accumulate three condos: one in Austin, Texas; one in Fort Lauderdale, Florida; and one in Memphis, Tennessee.

Karen has been very lucky in the sense that she has had good long-term tenants in all her condos. In fact, they were more like friends than tenants. Since Karen self-manages the properties, each year, she would do a site visit to the condos to check in.

However, Karen is deathly afraid of flying. She had a family member die in a plane crash years ago, and after that, she vowed never to travel by plane.

After Karen ended her consulting business, she moved permanently to Portland, Oregon. Her condos are all located quite far away from her current home, so Karen does a cross-country road trip each year to visit her properties and check on things. The good thing about this is that Karen doesn't mind the driving. In fact, she finds it therapeutic to get on the open road with some good music and a nice supply of snacks. After working with her for several years, we became accustomed to expecting very large car and travel expenses each year because of her annual trip to her properties.

As surprising as this may sound, Karen's travel costs to visit her rental properties are all tax deductible. Her trip is considered ordinary in nature because investors commonly visit their rental properties. Although driving from Portland, Oregon, to Austin, Texas, to do so is less common, that doesn't matter in this case, because it is still ordinary for Karen and her business.

The trip is necessary, because not checking on her properties and maintaining a good relationship with her tenants could be bad for Karen's business. Driving halfway across the country and back just to visit rental properties each year may sound strange, but for Karen, her trip expenses meet both the ordinary and necessary requirements to qualify as business deductions.

A business deduction can differ from one taxpayer to the next, because what is deductible for one person may not be deductible for another. It all depends on your situation and how each expense relates to your business.

For example, the United States Tax Court recently allowed a body builder to write off the cost of body oils, because this expense is common in his line of work. Given that body oils are required for competitions and are used by every competitor, he was able to claim the oils as an ordinary and necessary business expense. We real estate investors would definitely have a hard time arguing that we need body oils in our line of business, but for a body builder, it makes sense.

At the end of the day, what matters is the expense itself and how it could relate to your business. This doesn't mean, however, that you can't be creative with your deductions. There are many things that may not seem like obvious deductions, but if dealt with in the right way, they might just qualify. Let's take a look at some ways real estate investors could write off some wacky items.

Example 1: The Girlfriend

We can all agree that kids are very expensive, and some of you may agree that girlfriends can be equally expensive, if not more so. Here is a story of how one real estate investor was able to successfully write off the cost of his girlfriend.

This real estate investor owned a handful of rental properties and enjoyed spending time with his girlfriend so much that he decided they should work together. Rather than showering her with rare diamonds and gems, he gave her cash, the international language of love. But he didn't stop there. The savvy investor wanted to make sure that he got the IRS to help him pay for part of the money that he spends on his girlfriend. To do this, he legitimately hired his girlfriend to assist him with his rental properties—helping manage his rentals, picking up rent checks, furnishing his properties, and serving as his assistant. Because these were ordinary and necessary expenses for his real estate business, the IRS allowed this investor to write off the money spent, even though it was paid to his girlfriend.

Example 2: The Airplane

Sitting in traffic can be extremely boring and frustrating for anyone, especially if there is nothing good on the radio. Who (except our client Karen, of course) wants to sit in the car for five or six hours just to check on a rental property? What about sitting in traffic on the way to the airport, then standing in a long security line before squeezing into a tiny airplane seat for a few hours? That doesn't sound like much fun, either, does it?

Well, one successful real estate investor decided to take matters into his own hands. He was no longer going to waste time making the long drive to his rentals, nor was he going to squeeze in with the rest of us on a commercial flight. He and his wife went all out and invested in their own plane. Hey, if you have the money to buy and maintain a plane that can also be used as a tax write-off, why not?

Believe it or not, the Tax Court actually allowed this real estate couple to deduct their costs for this plane to visit their investment properties. Not only were they able to write off the cost of fuel and of hiring a pilot for these trips, but they were also able to write off a portion of the plane's depreciation. We primarily see people depreciating cars and RVs, and we can only imagine what that number looked like each year for depreciating a plane.

Example 3: Free Beer

Who doesn't love a good open house? Whether you are a real estate agent, investor, or flipper, there is something exciting about entering someone else's home to see how they live and to find inspiration on how to make a house a home. We see people do some crazy things at open houses nowadays. From catered food to celebrity appearances, these open house "parties" can get expensive quickly. Believe it or not, meals and entertainment are legitimate tax deductions that we commonly see missed on tax returns.

We met Jamie at a local real estate association meeting. She attended a presentation we gave about strategies to offset taxes on real estate commissions. When she showed up at our office a few months later, we were excited to take a look at her tax return from the prior year to see if there were any refund opportunities. Within the first three minutes of the meeting, we saw that her previous CPA may have missed something.

One of the first things we noticed is that she had claimed only a few hundred dollars for meal expenses. That didn't seem correct to us. Most real estate agents we know incur costs such as having coffee or a meal with clients as well as costs associated with open house activities. At first glance, it appeared that she might have the opportunity for a refund.

Now, you may already know that meals and entertainment can be tax deductible when they are business related. However, the IRS generally only allows us to write off 50% of these costs. For example, if you had a business meal with a client and spent $200, only $100 of that is tax deductible; the rest is not. A small loophole here is that if the meal is provided to the general public, then 100% of the cost is tax deductible. Generally, when you have an open house, you want everyone possible to show up, because you never know who your next buyer will be. It could be someone just driving by who saw your sign or the cousin of the nosy neighbor down the street.

In addition to the usual hors d'oeuvres and balloons you'd see at an open house, beer, wine, and any other alcohol provided are generally tax deductible. If you make the event open to the general public, you may be able to write off 100% of these alcohol expenses on your tax returns.

Because open houses are usually open to the general public, the expenses Jamie incurred for these events should have been 100% tax deductible rather than just 50% tax deductible. By understanding better which meals and entertainment can be deducted, Jamie is now able to capture her legitimate tax deductions for the first time.

Who knows, perhaps you'll want to go all out for your next open house now that you know dear old Uncle Sam will help you pay for it!

Example 4: Babysitting Fees
Every year, we probably have a few dozen clients who ask us whether

babysitting fees can be deducted as a business expense. Unfortunately, the general answer is no, they can't. As ridiculous as it may sound, the IRS sees babysitting fees as a personal expense, even if the fees were paid so that you could work on your real estate business. There are a few exceptions to this rule, though. We never give you bad news without also giving you potential strategies to deal with it!

We had a client, Eric, with a live-in nanny to whom he paid quite a bit of money each month. During the day, when the toddler was at preschool, the nanny would help Eric with profiling deals for his real estate business. Because part of the nanny's role was assisting with his business, a portion of what Eric paid her constituted a legitimate business expense he could deduct.

Even if the nanny did not provide any assistance to Eric with his real estate business, he could still claim a childcare tax credit for the money he paid her. This could be an option if Eric had to hire the nanny to watch the baby because both he and his wife worked during the day. However, this would not be directly related to the business and would therefore be only partially deductible on their personal returns.

Another potential way to write off babysitting fees is as a charitable donation. Eric and his wife were on the board of a nonprofit organization. The fees Eric pays a babysitter so he can leave the house and do volunteer work for a charity are deductible as charitable contributions. The charitable deduction strategy works even when you're not contributing directly to a charity. For example, if you wanted to roll up your sleeves to help your local Habitat for Humanity build a house, any sitter's fees you'd have to pay to do so would be tax deductible charitable donations.

What Does All This Mean?

Simply put, this means you can get creative with your taxes—within reason, of course. One mistake we see quite often is people not asking their CPA the right questions. Generally, people bring in a folder of tax documents and after chatting with their CPA about real estate, family, and the weather, ask something like, "Can I deduct my kids? They are growing up so fast and getting more and more expensive." The majority of the time, the answer will be no, you can't.

The correct question to ask in this situation is "How can I deduct my kids?" Simply adding a "how" at the beginning of the sentence prompts your CPA to think differently about the issue. In this situation, their response may be "Well, you can write off part of your car expenses if your kids are driving it around to help you with your real estate." The word "how" is extremely powerful, because it completely shifts your advisor's mind-set. This can turn a "no" into a "maybe," if not, hopefully, into a "yes." So the next time you meet with your CPA, be sure to begin your tax questions with "how."

A Clever Way to Write Off Your Kids

Day in and day out, your tax accountant can make or lose you more money than any single person in your life, with the possible exception of your kids
—Harvey Mackay

Ask any parent, and they may tell you that raising kids is life's biggest expense. When kids are young, the expenses may involve smaller items, such as diapers, pacifiers, and clothes. As kids become young adults, the costs can really start to grow. From cars to cell phones to college, kids can definitely be expensive. The IRS does offer some tax benefits for having kids in the form of tax exemptions and credits, but let's face it, those small benefits are nowhere close to the actual amount of money we spend on our kids over the course of a year. What if we could deduct some of the money we spend on our kids? Believe it or not, there are scenarios in which that can legitimately be done.

> **Real Life:** *Erin, like most moms, is excellent at multitasking. She juggles her day job, cleaning, cooking, and driving the kids to school and practice, as well as all the other things moms tend to manage. As if that weren't already enough, Erin also recently started investing in rental properties.*
>
> *Although she knew she probably wouldn't make a profit right away, when mortgage and repair expenses were high, she held on to*

the hope that her new properties would one day be profitable enough to bring in a little extra money and be a reliable source of additional income once retirement rolled around. Real estate was also something Erin had always wanted to do, but she had never had time to invest in it before, especially when her boys were little.

When Erin's boys, Jeremy and Jason, were in middle school and becoming ever more self-sufficient and independent, Erin decided it was a great time for her to finally start investing. The boys had reached an age where she felt comfortable leaving them at home alone for a few hours while she worked on her real estate investing business. When Erin purchased her first rental property, she figured she could get most of the required work done without having to drag her sons along with her every weekend. She never envisioned that her real estate work would become a way for her to bond with her kids.

Like most kids, if her boys wanted money for the weekend to see a movie with friends or buy a new video game, they had to earn it. If they washed the cars, did the dishes, or vacuumed the house, she would reward them with some cash. After she started her real estate business, there were even more opportunities for her sons to help out and earn some spending money.

When Jeremy and Jason were in middle school, they would help Erin by organizing the home office and by shredding papers. As they got older, their need for cash grew exponentially, thanks to sporting events, school dances, concerts, and all the other seemingly endless activities teenagers enjoy. Erin decided the boys were ready for bigger jobs and more responsibility, so she began giving them painting, gardening, and rental repair jobs. After tenants moved out, the boys were in charge of filling holes in the walls and putting on fresh paint. They even started to get handy by helping her install new cupboards and closet doors. They also helped with mowing lawns, trimming trees, and a few gardening projects. Because there wasn't always a job to do on the rentals, they would sometimes help around the office, taking checks to the bank and even assisting her with online advertising. Erin would never have admitted this, but she knew that both boys were much better than she was with computer-related tasks. She always had something her sons could help her with, and they were always eager to jump in. Over time, Erin's real estate venture *transitioned from an experiment into a real family business.*

After four years and five properties, Erin decided that she needed some tax advice and that it was time to hire a CPA. She was starting to make a significant profit on her rentals and wanted to make sure she was taking all the deductions she was entitled to. Erin knew she needed some professional advice if she was serious about keeping more of her profits.

We asked her if she paid her boys as employees. She explained that she generally paid them for completing tasks for her, but more like an allowance than a salary, because she didn't have any legitimate employees working for her business. We suggested that she should have some employees, specifically Jeremy and Jason. Now that her rentals were generating a profit instead of a loss, that profit could be taxed, and depending on her income, this could push her into a higher tax bracket for the year. This was exactly the bad news Erin had been hoping to avoid, so she was extremely excited to learn that there were some simple things she could do to prevent that from happening.

Shifting Income to Lower Tax Brackets

As part of our tax planning with Erin and her boys, we told her that paying her kids through the business rather than out of her own pocket would be very beneficial. When the boys are paid from the business account for work they did for the rental properties, the money may be documented as a business expense. The money would technically be considered wages at that point instead of an allowance. Erin was thrilled by this information, because she had not considered that deducting any of those expenses might be possible. She envisioned all the $20 bills she had constantly been handing her sons and wondered how much it would all total if she added it up. Once she was on board, we developed a plan with her.

The first step was to figure out how much she could reasonably justify as compensation for each boy. Reasonable compensation typically means "market rate." In other words, what would you pay someone else to do the task in question?

Based on the tasks and the abilities of each boy, we determined that paying them at a rate of $8 per hour was reasonable. Given that each boy worked about twelve hours a week, the total compensation she could reasonably pay them ended up being about $5,000 per child. Now she just had to make sure the money came out of the business account and not her personal cash. With this one strategy, Erin could essentially take a $10,000 allowance expense and make it a business expense instead. This would shift $10,000 from her 38% tax rate to her sons' 0% tax rate, reducing her overall taxes by close to $3,800!

Erin couldn't believe it. She was going to be getting an unexpected $10,000 tax write-off on money she was already giving her kids anyway!

Documentation, Documentation, Documentation

To do this properly, we recommended Erin put her kids on payroll. This meant setting up a payroll account with her local bank so that her boys could be paid each month and would receive a W-2 form at the end of the year. Each of the boys would then need to track their hours worked, along with a description of what was done. This could provide for proper documentation in the event of an audit. Although older kids can sometimes be paid as 1099 contractors, Erin would receive a better tax benefit by using the W-2 route, because her kids are both under the age of 18.

When we started talking about documentation, Erin suddenly had a few reservations about putting her kids on payroll. Jeremy was 16 and old enough to have a regular job, but Jason was only 14, and she was worried he was too young to actually work. Places such as restaurants and grocery stores have company rules stating the minimum age their employees must be. From what she had heard, even kids Jeremy's age had trouble finding a job with companies that hired people younger than 18.

This is a common concern, but the truth is that there is no age limit with regard to taxes. Infants perform in baby shampoo commercials, and toddlers model in Baby Gap catalogs, so hiring your children could be legal. The IRS does require that they be paid appropriately for the job, though. Your five year old is probably too young to help in your real estate business as a sales consultant, but an eleven or twelve year old is likely old enough to help with cleaning up your rental property. As long as Erin pays her kids appropriately for the tasks they do, their age doesn't matter to the IRS. Of course, Erin does need to make sure she follows her state's labor laws with respect to the number of hours and type of work appropriate for persons in that age group. Remember, just because they are your kids does not mean that you can ignore labor laws and work them to death with little or no pay.

Planning for the Kids' Futures

Another suggestion we had for Erin was to open a Roth IRA for each of her boys. As long as the kids were earning an income, they could contribute to a traditional or Roth IRA. These types of retirement accounts can offer great tax and investing benefits for such young people. For example, if Erin pays the boys $5,000 each year, that equals roughly $95 per week. If they spend $40 per week on food, movies, and friends, they can put the remaining $55 in their Roth IRA. Then all they have to do is sit back and watch it grow. Jeremy could have over $5,700 in his IRA before he even leaves for college, and Jason could have over $11,400 when he reaches that point. When the time rolls around to leave for college, the boys could withdraw money penalty free to pay for tuition, or if they waited a few more years, they could instead use the money for a down payment on their first home, again penalty free.

One of the best types of retirement accounts for kids is the Roth IRA, because it is a bucket of long-term, tax-free money that can be invested. The Roth IRA has huge growth potential, especially for young people, because they have plenty of time for the money to grow before an opportunity arises for them to use the funds.

Erin's next concern was that her older son would be going to college in a few years, and she wondered to what extent he could still be paid through the business. Jeremy hadn't applied to any schools just yet, but he had his sights set on one that was only about an hour away from their home. He would more than likely live on campus if he were accepted, because that is something he had always wanted to do, but he would very likely come home on most weekends as well as for holidays and summer break. We all agreed that it would be a great opportunity for him to help with Erin's rentals and could therefore still earn much of his allowance as a paycheck. He could even help with marketing from his dorm room if he wanted to. The possibilities were endless!

Erin left our meeting eager to make the new changes to make her sons legitimate employees of her real estate business. She knew they would both be very excited by the change and figured this would be another great learning opportunity for the boys with regard to managing money. Understandably, she was very excited about the newly discovered tax deductions, because she now had $10,000 to write off and exciting possibilities regarding her sons' futures.

It is important to note that there is also no maximum age limit with respect to hiring employees. We have several clients who hire their retired parents to help them with their business ventures.

One client, Jim, purchased a laundromat right around the time his mother was retiring. Not sure what to do with all her free time, his mom would go the laundromat each day and supervise, clean, and help out however she could. Because she insisted on being there every day to help, Jim decided to pay his mom a salary. The extra income was great for her, and Jim was able to take a tax deduction for it. In addition, he was able to deduct her medical expenses, because she was a legitimate employee. This helped increase his write-offs even more.

To be clear, your parents and children are not the only people who can be hired as your employees. Siblings, aunts, uncles, or anyone else willing to help with your real estate business may become your employees. There are potential employees everywhere. The people you hire just need to do work that is appropriate for their age and abilities and to be paid a reasonable amount for that work.

What Does All This Mean?

Having your kids or other family members help you with your real estate business may be both a great opportunity to teach them good habits and a valuable tax savings tool. By hiring them, you can potentially shift your income from your higher tax bracket to their lower tax bracket.

To ensure you are protected in case of an IRS audit, document all the work these individuals do for your business. Documentation is key when you hire family members, so be sure to record their pay and hours worked and maintain the appropriate payroll paperwork. Also remember that this income-shifting strategy is not limited to just your kids. If you have other family members helping in your real estate efforts, consider officially hiring them to increase your tax write-offs.

Writing Off Every Penny Of Your Vacation

The early bird catches the worm.

— Popular Proverb

Did you know that one person can deduct 100% of his vacation travel expenses while another person cannot deduct any of his vacation travel expenses? What if we told you that these two people traveled the same distance, paid the same costs, and even stayed at the same hotel? The truth is that it is possible for one person to have a tax-deductible vacation while another person's trip is completely nondeductible. The difference is how much proactive tax planning the traveler does before leaving on the trip.

What exactly is proactive tax planning? Simply put, proactive tax planning is when you meet with your tax advisor before making certain decisions to determine what actions you should take to reduce your taxes.

We are not talking about having taxes on your mind twenty-four hours a day, seven days a week. We are just talking about giving some thought to potential ways of saving taxes before you make certain business decisions.

How much does proactive tax planning help? Does it really work? The answer is yes. But don't just take our word for it. Let's take a look at how some very simple proactive planning can lead to significant tax savings and how a lack of planning can result in lost opportunities.

Proactive Planning

Real Life: One sunny January afternoon, our clients Ellen and Steve called us for a planning meeting. Usually our tax planning meetings consist of discussing entity strategies, payroll options for their business, or options for refinancing their rentals. But this meeting was very different. They explained to us that the weather in northern Washington state was very rainy, stormy, and cold—as it was every winter—and they wanted to come down to California for a few days for some sunshine. In fact, when Ellen called our office, her exact words were "Steve and I have not seen the sun in over ten days. I need to make a trip down to California to see you guys, and I need to know how to write off my trip."

It is always wonderful to see clients get to a point where they innately start to think about tax saving ideas as part of their daily life. Ellen and Steve had been clients of ours for years, and we were proud that this notion had finally kicked in for them.

Ellen told us that in addition to enjoying some nicer weather, she wanted to go to Universal Studios to see the shows and ride the rides. Another goal of hers was to attend a live taping of a TV show in Los Angeles (LA). Because she was fascinated with how celebrities live, she also wanted to go window shopping on Rodeo Drive, go on a star tour to see celebrities' homes, and visit the Hollywood Sign. If she had enough time, she really wanted to lie out on the beach and get a nice tan, too, so she could make her neighbors jealous when she returned home to Washington

This seemed like a tall order. Nowhere in that to-do list did we hear "real estate" or "taxes" or "business." Most, if not all, of the items on Ellen's list seemed like fun things she had planned for their trip.

However, with some preparation and a slight tweaking of their planned schedule, we found a pretty great solution.

Counting the Day

We explained that the best way to maximize Ellen and Steve's tax write-offs on this trip was to sandwich their fun weekend with business activities. They needed a reason to travel here besides the warm weather. So with a little

Internet research, Ellen found a real estate conference followed by a live taping of a real estate radio show that was happening on Friday in LA, and they signed up to go to it. They originally thought they would fly down on Thursday, attend the seminar on Friday, and then squeeze in Hollywood and a beach trip quickly on Saturday before flying back on Sunday afternoon.

We felt this was too rushed, plus, there were a bunch of things on Ellen's list that she wouldn't be able to fit in. This also left no time for them to meet with us to do some tax planning.

We suggested that they instead fly down on Thursday as planned and attend the seminar and radio show on Friday. Then they could sightsee and relax on both Saturday and Sunday. Lastly, they could have a tax planning meeting at our office on Monday and fly home on Tuesday.

This way, they could deduct all of their airfare, hotel, and rental car expenses, as well as 50% of their meals over six days without feeling like they were in California only to work. This is starting to sound more like a vacation now, right? Let's see exactly how this proactive planning worked out for them.

For you to deduct 100% of your travel expenses, such as airfare, hotels, and taxis, you must be able to show that the primary purpose of your trip was for business. The term "primary" simply means that more than 50% of your time is spent on business activities.

Travel days are considered business days by the IRS and are therefore tax deductible. Because Ellen and Steve flew in on a Thursday, that could be counted as a business day. Even though they arrived by noon on Thursday and spent the rest of the day and the evening lounging by the hotel pool and having dinner in town, it was still technically a business travel day.

On Friday, they attended the real estate conference for a few hours in the morning, ate lunch at a posh LA bistro on the way to their next event, and then wrapped up the day with a live taping of the real estate radio show. Friday was therefore considered a business day.

Saturday and Sunday were reserved for fun activities. This is when they did their Hollywood, Beverly Hills, and beach activities. These days would not be viewed as "business" days because they involved no business activities. However, the Monday tax-planning meeting allowed them to maximize their tax write-offs, because they sandwiched their fun weekend days between their business days.

Keep in mind that the bus tickets you buy for a tour of Hollywood and the money you pay to rent a surfboard at the beach are still nondeductible expenses. However, your meals for the weekend may still be tax deductible.

On Monday, they actually came to our office to discuss proactive tax planning for the rest of the year. We talked about all sorts of issues, from bad tenants and rehabbing nightmare stories to how to best preserve their assets for their grandson's college fund. Monday was therefore a business day.

After a nice dinner Monday evening, they went to bed and took the early flight home on Tuesday morning. Tuesday, of course, was thus another business day, because they had to travel home that day.

Weekend-Sandwich Strategy

Now you may not think that the meeting on Monday was all that important for Ellen and Steve, but that Monday meeting is what allowed them to write off their hotel, rental car, and food costs for the weekend. The only reason the hotel, rental car, and food costs on Saturday and Sunday were incurred was that they had a business reason to stay in Southern California until Monday: our tax-planning meeting. So, because they had business to do out of state both Friday and Monday, the weekend in between was eligible for tax deductions. This is what we CPAs commonly refer to as the "*weekend-sandwich strategy.*"

Now don't get us wrong, we did not lock Ellen and Steve up in our office for eight hours and force them to listen to us go on and on about all 600 pages of the latest changes to the tax code. We met for an hour and a half, had a nice working lunch, and before they knew it, there were back at their hotel, drinking cocktails by the pool.

Without this Monday meeting, they may have lost out on the ability to deduct some of their weekend expenses. They may have received deductions for only half of their trip if not for this strategically planned tax meeting.

Audit Protection

One of the main things you can do to protect yourself from an audit is to have the right kinds of documentation in place. With regard to travel costs, the primary thing the IRS looks for is "business purpose." The best way to prove your business purpose is to show that you had predetermined business activities, meetings, or events set up. These things must therefore be arranged before you leave on your trip.

For example, Ellen and Steve registered for the real estate conference before they left on their trip. They have emails from us to confirm that a tax meeting was scheduled before their departure. The documentation for both of these things can prove that there was a predetermined business purpose for the trip. Technically, Steve and Ellen had to have a hotel room on both Saturday and Sunday night because they were waiting for their tax-planning meeting on Monday. This is how Steve and Ellen were able claim that their trip was "primarily for business."

On the other hand, if Ellen and Steven had simply bought their plane tickets to California, stopped by a real estate conference after seeing it on a billboard, and hopped over to our office on their way to the beach, this would not have qualified their trip as a business trip for tax purposes. In that case, they would have been on vacation and just happened to do some business-related things. In other words, they incurred the flight and hotel costs because of their California vacation, so those costs may not be deductible as business expenses.

So, as you can see, a few small action items before leaving on a trip can make all the difference with respect to tax deductions. A little bit of proactive tax planning can result in thousands of dollars in tax savings.

All in all, Ellen and Steve were able to write off a very large portion of their travel expenses for this trip. Not only did they accomplish all the items on their to-do list, but they also ended up with about $2,700 worth of tax write-offs. Essentially, they got a 50% discount on their travel using the appropriate tax loopholes provided by Uncle Sam. Not bad for a little bit of proactive planning, right?

What Could Happen Without Proactive Planning?

Now what if someone were to travel without proactive tax planning? Could it really make a big difference? Let's consider another client of ours named Tim and what happened when he attended a friend's wedding in Florida without proactive planning.

Real Life: *Tim received a wedding invitation from a college buddy and flew to Florida for a week over the summer to attend the wedding and visit with family. When the family dinners and wedding were over and the rest of the family had returned to their respective states, Tim spent the remaining days of his trip in his hotel room, answering emails and phone calls and catching up on business. Although he ultimately spent about 80% of his time in Florida working, Tim would later find out that none of his travel, meal, or hotel expenses were deductible, because he did not have any predetermined business purposes for his trip. The original purpose of his trip was not work, even though he spent majority of it actually working.*

This is not all bad news, though. Tim could still deduct the cost of his hotel Wi-Fi, printing, faxes, and a business book he bought to read on the flight—but that was all.

Now we know you must be thinking, "Why was Tim's trip not deductible if he spent most of it working?"

Well, the reason is that the IRS determines whether a trip is deductible based on the purpose of the travel. In this example, the purpose of Tim's travel was to attend a friend's wedding in Florida. While on this trip, he just happened to work from his hotel, check email, and speak to clients. His flight to Florida, hotel stay, and meals were all nondeductible because he did not need to incur these expenses to work. He could have very well stayed at home or gone to his office to do the same work he did from his hotel room, right? If not for his friend's wedding, Tim would have been at home and never would have needed to incur any hotel or flight expenses.

We have now presented two similar trips with two very different tax implications. This shows the power of proactive tax planning. You can see how with a little bit of proactive planning and a little help from your CPA, you can use these IRS rules to your advantage and return from your trip feeling relaxed, refreshed, and even a little richer.

What Does All This Mean?

A little planning can go a long way in the tax world. As we look at ways to minimize our taxes, everyday decisions such as vacation and travel plans may be opportunities for us to save money.

The key to maximizing your tax deductions for vacation travel is to document your business activities for the trip. To simply be "working" while you are traveling is not enough. The IRS needs to see a predetermined business reason for why you are traveling in the first place. This is one of the main reasons doing some proactive planning before leaving on your trip can be significantly helpful.

Remember, the IRS rewards planning, not spontaneity. So be sure to schedule meetings and other business activities before you leave on your next trip, and record all your expenses and tax write-offs while you are away. You can still enjoy your vacation and travel as you incorporate business and investing elements into the mix. The bonus is that you may have enlisted Uncle Sam's help in funding your vacation.

Maximizing Your Write Offs of Travel Expenses

Few of us ever test our powers of deduction, except when filling out an income tax form.

– Laurence J. Peter

Have you ever traveled to a beautiful location such as Hawaii or the Caribbean and thought about how wonderful owning rental properties there would be? Ever wonder whether buying an investment property there might allow you to write off your travel costs to return there in the future?

A similar scenario we see quite a bit is investors owning properties in locations where they have family and friends. It is common for someone to own property in their hometown, where their parents have retired, or invest in cities where their kids and/or grandkids live. Of course, if you own a property in a different state that is near a family member or loved one, odds are you would want to spend a few extra travel days there when visiting your property so you could have some quality time with those individuals, right? In those scenarios, how can you be sure to maximize your tax deductions as real estate investors? Let's consider some options.

> **Real Life:** *We met Dave and Denise a few years ago at one of our educational Saturday brunches. They had both retired about five years earlier and started to invest in real estate almost right away.*

They had always wanted to get involved with real estate, but with raising two kids and working full-time, they had never really gotten around to doing it before.

They had purchased about a dozen single-family homes since their retirement and were looking to expand and buy a few more. To our surprise, Dave and Denise were not locals like most of our brunch attendees. They were actually from central California, and had driven almost five hours to Orange County to attend our brunch and sharpen their real estate skills.

Over the next year, they came to two more brunch events as well as a few real estate investor meetings (all in Orange County), and whenever we saw them, they would give us an update on their adventures and their grandchildren. It was a pleasant surprise when they called our office in late January and asked us to prepare their tax returns that year.

We realized that Dave and Denise were extremely organized when we got all their documents in the mail. Every property income and expense sheet was paper clipped with its respective 1099 and mortgage interest statements. Despite their great record keeping, however, we noticed that one huge thing was missing from their paperwork—travel expenses.

Dave and Denise had properties in five different states. Because they were new to real estate investing, they liked to keep track of how each of their properties was doing. It was common for them to drive back and forth between central California, Arizona, and Nevada several times a year to take care of some of their closer rentals. In addition, they drove about 450 miles round trip several times a year to attend real estate conferences in Southern California.

Even though Dave and Denise did not provide us with any travel expenses, we knew they must have had some. Just based on our casual conversations with them and their attendance at our brunch events, we knew that this was a potentially big tax saving area they might have missed.

We called Denise to ask whether she perhaps forgot to include these expenses. Not surprisingly, her response was the same one we've heard so many times before: "I didn't know I could deduct that."

We explained to Denise that any travel expenses directly related to business or real estate could be tax deductible. As long as they are visiting their rentals, scoping out new ones, or attending conferences related to real estate, pretty much all their travel related expenses could be accounted for come tax time.

The most common travel expense, of course, is cars. Generally, travel-related car expenses are deductible. This can include oil changes, maintenance, gas, repairs, parking, tolls, and depreciation. It is important to hold on to your receipts and keep a travel log so your CPA can calculate how much of these expenses can be used to offset your taxes each year. However, if you have a separate car used exclusively for business, all these expenses may be deducted on your tax returns.

Train and airfare tickets are also deductible, plus any baggage fees you incur while traveling. Keep in mind, though, that these expenses need to be within reason, so you can't necessarily fly first class all over the country just to "look at real estate" and expect to write off all your travel costs.

Here's a tip: if you really do want that first class ticket for your six- or seven-hour flight, deduct the price of what the economy ticket would cost, and pay the difference for the first class ticket out of your personal account, rather than your business account. For example, let's say that an economy-class ticket for a round-trip flight between Los Angeles and New York costs $800, but a first class ticket costs $1,200. Technically, the $800 would be a business expense, and the $400 difference would be considered a personal expense. Therefore, you could still purchase the first class ticket and write off $800. Depending on your income tax rate, this could save you $400 or more in taxes.

Taxi, subway, and bus expenses are also deductible when you are traveling for business purposes. Although these may seem to be small expenses, they can add up very quickly, especially if you are traveling around a busy city, and can become real cash savings for you at tax time. Be sure to track these expenses in your QuickBooks, a log, or a journal, because receipts are not given in most of these cases. And if you liked a particular taxi driver or baggage attendant, don't forget to tip them—tips are tax deductible, too!

Given that Uncle Sam is sharing the cost of your business travel with you, these are times when it makes sense to spend a little extra (within reason, of course). You may not want to rent a Lamborghini, but maybe a little convertible would be a nice treat. After all, if you are traveling out of town to meet with investors, it makes sense to show up in style, right? So perhaps on your next business trip, you can ditch the bus or cab and rent a sports car instead!

Overnight lodging is another deductible business travel expense. This includes room service, Wi-Fi, tips, valet parking fees, and even the cost of sending your suits out for dry cleaning. Often, when you attend a large real estate conference, the company hosting the event will negotiate group rates with local hotels. These are usually great opportunities to be close to the conference and mingle with other investors even after the event is over for the day. The hosts, however, may pick some of the pricier hotels in the area. You generally things don't want to miss out on these opportunities, though, so book the hotel, save your receipts, and deduct your expenses on your tax return.

In addition to travel, lodging, and auto expenses, one deduction many real estate investors miss is a meals and entertainment write-off. Keep in mind that this is a 50% deduction, but when you need to eat out several times a day, this expense can add up very quickly. Perhaps you go to Las Vegas for a seminar or real estate conference. In addition to your lodging and travel expenses, if you plan your weekend just right, you can also deduct shows, movies, buffets, and dinners. As always, don't forget to keep your receipts. The tax code states that receipts must be kept for any entertainment expense over $75. When tax time rolls around, provide information on the full amount of your meals and entertainment expenses to your CPA, and they will apply the 50% rule. Otherwise, you might miss out on some deductions.

Real estate and educational meetings are deductible as well, and not just the registration fee. Travel to and from the event is deductible, as well as any of the aforementioned expenses. Maybe you saw an ad for a business management or real estate conference in Hawaii. Perhaps this could be your chance for a business vacation with a few days of real estate education and a weekend of beaches, spas, and luaus.

When we began to explain these rules to Denise, she was very adamant that these deductions did not apply to her. She explained that they strategically picked their rentals based on where their kids and grandkids lived. When they drove to Los Angeles or flew to Pennsylvania, they were visiting their properties and attending meetings and seminars, but they usually also took time to see their family. This is why Denise felt their expenses wouldn't be deductible.

Unfortunately, this is a myth we hear time and time again. Just because you stop in to see family or friends on your way to visit a rental property, that doesn't mean the travel cost is not deductible. It is very possible to write off your travel costs, even if you take a day or a weekend to visit with family en route.

After hearing Denise's reasons for not sending us her travel expenses, we explained that as long as the primary reason for their trip is business, they can deduct the associated travel expenses. Furthermore, even if the primary reason for a trip was to visit family, and she spent only a little bit of time on her rental properties, some of her travel and out-of-pocket costs might still be legitimate tax write-offs.

Denise was shocked. She and Dan had been in real estate for five years and never realized how many deductions they were missing out on. She assumed that because part of their travel time was spent with family, none of their expenses could be deducted, when in reality, most of it could because the primary reason for their travel was their rentals. They often traveled if there was a problem with one of their properties, if they needed to meet someone, or they were looking for a new property. Generally, only after all the work had been taken care of would they head over to see their grandkids.

The Weekend Sandwich

We also gave them a few planning ideas so they could ensure that for the next year, their travels would be deductible. One method is to plan meetings on a Thursday and Friday, spend Saturday and Sunday with the family, and then conclude the trip with property viewings on Monday and Tuesday. By sandwiching personal activities between business activities, you can maximize your tax deductions and even make part of your weekend expenses tax deductible as well.

The Standard Deduction

For the first year, we used a standard deduction for Dave and Denise's auto expenses, because they had not kept receipts for gas, repairs, or parking. The IRS actually introduced this method, believe it or not, which allows you to take a deduction based on your mileage. For this deduction, you simply multiply the number of miles driven for business by the IRS's standard reimbursement rate. For example, in 2015, the standard amount was 57.5 cents per mile. So, for each round trip of 450 miles between central and Southern California, Dave and Denise could deduct $258.75. Multiply that by three real estate conference trips, and that is a total of $776 on mileage alone. On top of that, they were able to deduct hotel expenses, the price of the conferences, and 50% of their meals and entertainment.

That year, after scrambling to find every travel receipt they could from their trips, Dave and Denise ultimately accumulated almost $3,500 in travel expenses. The following year, with better record keeping and knowledge of how and what to deduct, they were able to account for over $5,000 in travel expenses. This goes to show that knowing what you can deduct can make a huge difference in your tax savings!

What Does All This Mean?

Contrary to popular belief, the IRS is not as terrible as one may think. A lot of loopholes are written into the tax code that taxpayers are invited to use. As you can conclude from Dave and Denise's story, the IRS does allow tax deductions even when business travel includes certain personal benefits. As long as the primary purpose of a trip is business related, you may still write off certain travel expenses.

Many times, we've heard investors complain about not wanting to keep track of car and other travel costs because doing so is a hassle. However, by putting certain systems in place, your record keeping can be highly automated. Once you start really tracking your business expenses when you travel to take care of your properties, you will see how quickly they can add up. Remember, a penny saved is a penny earned, so hold on to your hardearned money. Next time you travel for your real estate business, try to use the "weekend sandwich" strategy to squeeze in some weekend fun on Uncle Sam's dime.

Squeezing the Most Benefit from Your Home Office

There's no place like home.

– L. Frank Baum
The Wonderful Wizard of Oz

In 2013, *Forbes* magazine estimated that of the roughly 26 million Americans who have home offices, only 3.4 million claim these legitimate expenses on their taxes. That means that almost 87% of people with a home office may be missing out on home office deductions! Considering that the average home office creates write-offs between $2,000 and $3,000, this means billions of dollars are missed each year. So the natural question is why are so many people not taking this deduction? There are actually two main reasons:

1. Bad guidance from conservative tax advisors

2. Not knowing what qualifies as deductible

We once read a letter from a tax advisor to their client that went something like this:

"Caution: be wary of the home office deduction. On Wednesday at 4 a.m., a local Arizona man and his family were awakened when S.W.A.T broke down his front door and barged in to arrest the taxpayer for taking a home office deduction on his tax return."

Now, you may be surprised to hear that we were not scared by this letter at all. In fact, it was pretty clear to us that the letter was not based on any factual information. The scariest part of this letter was that it was actually being sent to a taxpayer by their tax advisor.

If you are one of the millions of people who have been told that you should not take a home office deduction because of IRS audits, you are not alone. This is one of the most common myths in the tax world today. The truth is that the home office deduction has not been a high audit area for over a decade. In fact, in recent years, the IRS has made it even easier to standardize ways this legitimate tax deduction can be taken. Yet surprisingly, millions of Americans still fall victim to the old scare tactics and don't take the deductions they are legally entitled to. How beneficial can a home office deduction really be? Let's take a look at the correct way to use this tax deduction.

> **Real Life:** *After completing many years of schooling to get her engineering degree, our client Ali came to the unfortunate conclusion that she didn't love her engineering job as much as she thought she would. Having burnt out at work, and in an effort to phase out of her W-2 job, Ali began investing in real estate. She jumped right in, purchasing four rental properties within her first year of investing. She rented a two-bedroom apartment at the time and used the second bedroom as her home office, from which she ran her growing real estate business. Until that point, she had always done her tax returns herself with TurboTax. But now with all her new properties, she wasn't quite sure how to report everything and didn't want to risk doing them incorrectly herself, so she decided to have us help her with her taxes.*
>
> *After reviewing all her tax documents, we noticed that Ali was missing her home office deduction expenses. We knew that she didn't have a separate office space for her real estate business, so she had to be working from somewhere. After speaking to Ali, we realized that she had no idea that she could take a deduction for her home office. She was under the assumption that she could not take a home office deduction, because her engineering day job was where her primary office was. Ali was curious as to exactly how the home office deduction works and what the rules were to writing things off legally.*

What You Need to Know to Write Off Your Home Office

The most common reason for missing out on a home office deduction is the ever-looming fear of an IRS audit. Many tax advisors have very conservative habits with respect to tax deductions. Because home offices at one time (more than ten years ago!) were a red flag for the IRS, preparers still dissuade clients from taking the deductions. However, with millions of Americans now working from home, it no longer stands out as a suspicious deduction to the IRS. In fact, the IRS has actually made it easier for taxpayers to deduct this legitimate write-off.

There are, however, a few rules and limitations to know when claiming a home office on your returns. For one, the space must be your primary place of business. If you work your day job from an office building and occasionally do work at home after hours, you may not qualify for the home office deduction. However, if you work from home most of the time, perhaps because you don't have a separate office space, you may be able to take the tax deduction. You may also qualify for the deduction by working mostly from home and visiting the office only occasionally to meet with clients. Or perhaps you are a telecommuter and only visit the office for a monthly meeting or to check in with your supervisor.

Even though Ali's main place of work for her engineering business was in an office, her home office was still her "primary place of business" for her real estate activities. Because she did not have another primary place to conduct her real estate business, she met the primary place of business requirement for her home office.

You may still be able to take a home office deduction, even if you have another office. Say you work from home, but you also rent a second office space that you use to meet with clients in a professional setting. Your home office may still be deductible, because it is your principal place of business, and you use the second office only occasionally.

Secondly, the part of your home that you use as your home office must be used exclusively for business purposes. You can't use the kitchen table as your home office, because more than likely, you also eat dinner there. The same goes for your living room couch. You may answer most of your emails from the couch, but chances are that you also use that space to entertain or to watch television. Your home office needs to be a space that is set aside only for work. For example, as we mentioned earlier, many investors use a spare bedroom as their home office, or they may have a desk area set up in one specific part of their home. As long as both requirements are met (primary and exclusive area for business), the home office deduction may be claimed on your returns. But make sure that if necessary, you can prove that your workspace is your primary place of business and used exclusively for your business. When trying to prove that you have a legitimate home office, pictures can often help.

Not Knowing What Qualifies as Deductible Items

Another reason many taxpayers ignore the home office deduction is that they just don't know they can take it. Some have no idea that it's available to them, and others simply assume they don't qualify.

Home Office Myths

One home office myth is that the space must be a fully enclosed, separate room. In fact, the IRS simply requires that the home office be a dedicated space that is used just for your business. For example, you may have a sitting area in your master bedroom that has a desk, chair, and filing cabinets for all your real estate files. That could qualify as a defined "space" that is dedicated as a home office. So, part of a spare room or even the end of a hallway may be a legitimate tax deduction, as long as it is used exclusively for business.

Another common myth is that you have to have a net profit to take the deduction. In reality, it is sometimes possible to take a home office deduction even when there is no net profit on the tax return. Strategies using legal entities such as S corporations can help companies that are losing money still get a tax deduction for home office write-offs.

Now that we have dispelled some of the most common myths about home office deductions, let's consider some of the ways you can write off your home office expenses.

The Actual Expense Method

The actual expense method allows you to deduct a portion of your home expenses as business expenses, depending on the size of your home workspace. Some common expenses you can claim on your tax returns are mortgage interest, property tax, homeowners association dues, and homeowners insurance. In addition, the cost of cleaning, utilities, phone service, Internet, and even security or alarm systems may be partially deducted as part of home office expenses. Last but not least, maintenance, pest control, repair, and home improvement costs may also be used as write-offs for your business.

What most people do not know is that even if you do not own your home and are simply renting an apartment, you may still benefit from the home office write-off by deducting a portion of your rent and renter's insurance.

Keep in mind that when you take a home office deduction using the actual method for mortgage interest, property taxes, or mortgage insurance premiums, this reduces the amount reported as itemized deductions on your personal tax returns. For example, if you paid $10,000 in mortgage interest during the year and deducted $2,000 as a home office expense for your real estate business, only the remaining $8,000 can be reported as an itemized deduction on your personal taxes.

Direct Versus Indirect

Another distinction to understand when writing off home office expenses is the difference between direct and indirect expenses. With indirect expenses, such as rent, mortgage interest, utilities, and property taxes, only a portion of each can be deducted for business use. For example, if you use one of the five rooms in your home for your real estate work, you can generally deduct only 20% of these expenses for your business. However, some expenses may instead be classified as direct expenses, if they apply specifically to the home office portion of the house. Examples of direct expenses are painting the room where your home office is located, paying a handyman to install bookshelves or a desk, and replacing a window in the office itself. The great thing about direct expenses is that they are generally 100% deductible, whereas indirect expenses are usually only partially deductible.

The Simplified Method

There is yet another reason home office deductions are missed: many business owners don't keep records of their home expenses. Maybe you don't feel like checking all your statements and bills to calculate how much you spent on utilities, insurance, and repairs. If so, you're in luck! In recent years, the

IRS has made claiming a home office deduction even easier, which further supports our claim that taking the deduction no longer triggers a red flag for an audit.

The new simplified method allows you to deduct $5 for each square foot of home office space. For example, if you use a 100-square-foot area of your spare room as your workspace, you may be able to take a $500 deduction. However, using the simplified method means that you generally cannot take any additional write-offs related to your home office, such as cleaning, repairs, or insurance. Property taxes and mortgage interest are still deductible on your personal tax return, so in a way, the simplified method allows you to double dip a little of your expenses. Keep in mind, though, that the simplified method is a substitute for calculating actual expenses, not an addition to your other expenses.

This rule has limits, however, and there is a maximum deduction of $1,500, which corresponds to 300 square feet. As we discussed earlier, the average home office generates between $2,000 and $3,000 in write-offs, so the simplified method doesn't always guarantee maximum tax deductions. If you are not great with bookkeeping and tracking expenses, or if you are preparing your returns at the last minute and don't have time to add everything up, this method can be very helpful for claiming some last minute write-offs.

Now that you have the basics, let's get back to our story about Ali. We asked her to gather any documents applicable to her home office, so she went through her receipts and bank statements and was able to pull together all her apartment-related expenses for the year. Because she used one of the four rooms in her apartment as her home office (the total number of rooms included the kitchen and living room), she was able to deduct 25% of her rent, insurance, cleaning, utilities, Internet, and phone costs as legitimate business expenses.

In the end, by claiming a home office deduction, Ali was able to write off about $4,000, which saved her almost $1,200 in taxes. What is so wonderful about the home office deduction is that the strategy did not cost Ali any additional money. It simply allowed a lot of her personal nondeductible expenses to be claimed as legitimate tax write-offs.

The home office deduction is a great loophole that can help you take thousands of dollars of write-offs for your business, without spending any extra money. Home repairs, cleaning, and all the other items we've noted are generally expenses you would pay for anyway, so why not deduct as much of those expenses as you can?

Make sure to work with a CPA who is on your side and willing to take the deduction for all your legitimate expenses. There's no need to leave money on the table when you can write off every dollar you are entitled to.

What Does All This Mean?

Back in ancient times, many believed the Earth to be flat. Wouldn't it be silly for someone to make that claim today knowing that there is plenty of evidence to support the earth is the shape of a sphere? This is just one example of a myth that held some power long ago but that really has no validity in today's world. The same can be said for the home office deduction when it comes to high IRS audit risk.

As taxpayers, we need to be aware of the tax deductions we are legally entitled to. By succumbing to outdated scare tactics the IRS propagated decades ago, we are giving more of our hard-earned money to the IRS than we need to. As archaic and bureaucratic as the IRS may be, it has publicly recognized that home office deductions are now more common than ever before. Surprisingly, it has even taken steps to help taxpayers claim that legitimate deduction by providing an easy and standardized way of writing off our home office expenses. If you are someone with a legitimate home office and have not been taking advantage of this option in the past, ask yourself, "What is stopping me from taking that deduction this year?"

Don't fall victim to the myths and superstitions about the home office deduction. If you qualify, take it!

ENTITIES

Your Legal Entities the Right Way

My limited liability company protected me from an expensive lawsuit, even though I never used it for my real estate.

— No One (Ever!)

If you went to see your doctor about a bacterial infection, and he prescribed you antibiotics, would you expect to get better by not taking the medication? Probably not. Then why do we set up legal entities for asset protection without actually using them to protect ourselves? That is the million-dollar question. Now you may think we are being facetious, but the truth is that we meet dozens and dozens of investors each year who are victims of this false sense of security, which usually manifests in one of the following two ways:

1. Not using the legal entities the way they were intended to be used

2. Not using the legal entities at all after they have been set up

Many people really do create legal entities to protect their assets and save taxes but don't actually do anything with the entities after they've been formed. Once the attorney has been paid to establish the entities, the beautiful, leather-bound entity binders sit unused on a shelf, simply gathering dust. In addition, the unused entity itself may be accruing costs each year. Many investors are under the impression that once the entity exists, somehow they just magically receive the related tax and asset protection benefits. This couldn't be further from the truth.

If you own an entity or are planning to create one, you need to make sure that your entity actually does what you put it in place to do. If you set up a partnership or corporation and then never put it to work, you likely have a false sense of security, because you are probably not actually protected from lawsuits and taxes.

> **Real Life:** *We have a friend named Andy who, unfortunately, is a perfect example of this problem. Andy is a seasoned real estate investor of almost a decade who owns about a dozen properties. Andy is actively involved in investor circles and communities, offering help and advice to others about their real estate ventures. He is always exploring innovative new ways to invest and sharing his success stories.*
>
> *Andy called us recently to ask if we could help him with a bit of tax planning. He was in the process of purchasing a few new rentals and wanted to know if he needed to set up a new entity to hold them or if he could use an existing partnership that he already owned. He had had an attorney create several entities for him years earlier, but he had not done any planning or maintenance since then and wanted us to take a look to ensure that things were still going well.*
>
> *Unfortunately for Andy, things were not going well. We reviewed Andy's properties, looked at his prior year tax returns, and realized that he had filed six no activity returns in the previous two years and paid over $6,000 in accounting fees. This told us that Andy had six entities that held no real estate, made no money, and provided him with no tax or asset protection benefits.*
>
> *At this point, Andy did not need new entities; he needed to sort out the ones he already had. We noticed that Andy was still reporting his rental income and expenses on his personal returns and that tenants were writing their rent checks to him personally. The worst part was that Andy was unaware that he was not using his entities correctly. He was under the assumption that he had already done what was necessary to protect his investments and minimize his taxes.*
>
> *As strange as it may sound, an entity with no activity is losing money, even without any income or expense transactions. Andy was losing lots of money through his no activity entity, including hundreds of dollars for legal set-up and maintenance costs, as well as tax return filing costs each year. Such expenses can add up to hundreds, or even*

thousands, of dollars for an entity that is not making any money to offset them.

We explained to Andy that for the entities to work the way they should, he needed to treat them as separate entities rather than having everything jumbled together in his personal accounts.

That meant opening bank accounts for his limited liability companies (LLCs) and perhaps also getting a debit or credit card to go along with each one. From that point forward, when he bought paint or new blinds or anything else his rentals needed, he would incur the expense under his business's name instead of his own. So remember that if you set up a business account, be sure to use it! You don't want it to sit around unused, simply accumulating fees.

Warning Signs

If you file a no activity tax return, this generally means that you have created an entity that is doing absolutely nothing. It is not holding properties, it is not generating revenue, and it is not paying business expenses. If you are filing a no activity tax return, you need to meet with your advisor to discuss ways to best use your entity. If that entity is not ultimately needed and not benefiting you, work with your advisor to dissolve it altogether.

Occasionally, though, having an entity with no income or expenses can make sense. Perhaps you formed a partnership in early December but didn't quite get all your assets in place by year-end. You may not show any income or expenses in that year, because you had only a few weeks in which to do so. This is a common occurrence and generally not a problem. If you're in your second year of business, however, and your LLC still has no income or expenses, you definitely need to do some planning with your tax advisor.

When you are establishing a legal entity, the goal is generally to either protect your assets, minimize your taxes, or both. In addition to setting it up correctly, here are some ways you can make sure you are using your entities correctly to get the most tax and asset protection benefits.

Keep Business and Personal Expenses Separate

Occasionally, you may forget your business credit/debit card at home and have to pay for something business related from your personal account. In that case, be sure to reimburse yourself from the company so that all business expenses are accounted for in your books. However, if you forget your personal debit/credit card at home, don't use your business card to cover any personal expenses. That could cause problems if you are involved in litigation or an IRS audit, and it is just a bad business habit in general. Be sure to use the proper card for the corresponding account whenever possible. This will also minimize the pain and time needed to separate your real estate expenses from your personal expenses at tax time.

If you have multiple properties held under one entity, make sure to keep track of which property each expense is for. Write the address of the rental at the top of the receipt, or keep receipts in their own separate file folder until you can enter them into Excel or QuickBooks. When the time comes to prepare your tax returns, you will need to provide expenses for each entity and a detailed breakdown for each property.

Having separate bank accounts can help you tremendously for audit protection purposes. The IRS generally puts more weight on something being a business expense if it has been paid for out of a legitimate operating legal entity's account rather than an individual's personal bank account. This offers more clarity as to why the expenses were incurred. If you sat down with an auditor and showed them your personal bank statements, defending why certain expenses were business related instead of personal might be a bit of a challenge. An expense at Lowe's could be a personal expense if you were improving your primary home. How would you prove that such an expense was related to a rental property and not your personal home? If all your expenses for your entity were on one standalone business bank account statement, it would be much easier to show that they were business related.

Another good idea is to obtain a business checkbook, so you don't write any personal checks for business expenses. First, you do not want to give a check with your home address on it to an outside contractor. They are working for your business, not for you. Second, what if the check bounces? You may be personally liable for repayment and penalties instead of your business, which should have issued the check in the first place. Having digital or carbon copies or check stubs can be helpful when year-end and tax season come around, so you have a paper trail of your check recipients and dates. Use the check's memo line to record the type of repair, improvement, or expense being paid, as well as which property it corresponds to. This way, you can clearly show why you made each payment, not only for the IRS, but also for your own records.

Putting Your Business In Charge of Business

Most people who form legal entities do so for asset protection purposes. However, your business can't protect your assets if those assets are still in your name personally! In addition to business accounts, you need to transfer real estate titles to your entity. If you are sued by a tenant or property manager, they can legally go after the person or entity whose name is on the title, and if that is your name, they may be able to take away your personal assets if you are otherwise unable to pay. As you can see, making sure your business legally owns your real estate is extremely important. Any entity set up to hold a property but that doesn't actually hold the title is useless.

In addition, any rent received should flow through your business. Rather than your tenants writing "Pay to the Order of John Smith" on their checks, they should write "Pay to the Order of ABC Company." If your entity's name is on the property's title and on the corporate card, it also needs to be on the rent checks. This will help with personal protection, as discussed earlier, and will also make bookkeeping much easier if you are depositing rent checks into your business account.

If you happen to have an S corporation and are not using it correctly— for example, by using it to pay for personal expenses—you can actually have your S corporation election cancelled by the IRS without warning. They could even change the company to a C corporation, which may be subject to more taxes and even double taxation!

While separating your business and personal accounts may seem like common sense, not doing so is actually a mistake we see all the time. Andy is just one of the dozens and dozens of investors we meet who make mistakes with respect to their legal entity. Believe it or not, and to our continued horror, he is also one of dozens of investors who still, despite our constant warnings, use this single-account business plan, living each day with a false sense of security. If a tenant were to file a lawsuit related to one of his properties, Andy could be sued personally, because his name is the one on the title and on the rent checks. We have clients who continue to use their personal accounts to pay for everything, even after being informed of the pitfalls of this way of doing business. We even have some clients who use one business account to pay for everything, including personal expenses, which is even worse!

For some, separating expenses or tracking each company in a different QuickBooks file may seem like too much work. Hiring a bookkeeper may be a worthwhile investment, but at the end of the day, the business owner must make the necessary changes to ensure that they are properly protected from lawsuits and prepared for potential audits. In short, make sure your entity is actually performing the functions you set it up to do.

What Does All This Mean?

Simply owning a property does not automatically mean it will generate rental income. You must lease the property to another person and take steps to ensure that it is an income-generating asset. Similarly, simply owning a legal entity does not automatically provide an investor with any asset protection. The entity must be used correctly for its intended purpose. To ensure that you are getting the intended liability protection and tax savings from your legal entity, work with your advisors to ensure that the entity properly holds the title(s) to your property.

Remember, having separate bank accounts, debit cards, and checkbooks for your entity and for your personal expenses is also important. Have rent checks written out and addressed to your entity, and pay all your business expenses from your entity's accounts. Essentially, treat the entity as separate from your personal activities to ensure protection.

If you are not using your existing entities, talk to your CPA as soon as possible about taking the necessary steps to ensure your entities are doing what they have been set up to do.

Legal Entity Lies Exposed

Never spend your money before you have it.

— Thomas Jefferson

There is something almost sexy about being a business owner. Being able to hand out a business card that says

John Smith

President and CEO

Evergreen Real Estate Global, Inc.

Sort of makes one feel like a real estate mogul, doesn't it? Although legal entities can provide investors with some benefits, they usually also come at a cost.

As real estate investors, we should make many of our decisions as business decisions. That means analyzing and considering both the cost and the benefit of each transaction. Sometimes we may be so excited about a new real estate venture that we don't take the time to fully determine the best structure for that specific transaction.

__Real Life:__ Jeff loved playing Monopoly as a kid. That was actually how he became interested in real estate. He loved seeing the board fill up with little red and green houses, and he loved that he could charge people who landed on his squares rent. In real life, Jeff worked as a server at a high-end restaurant. His favorite thing to do on a work night was come home and watch watch reality TV shows about real estate investing. Jeff's mantra was always "One day...." One day he would own real estate, one day he would be wealthy, and one day he may even have a real estate show of his own.

At the age of forty-five, Jeff did not yet own any investment properties, but he had dedicated quite a bit of time to educating and preparing himself to do so. Jeff traveled across the United States and took countless classes to learn about rental real estate, tax liens, note buying, and apartment investing. Jeff also attended his local real estate club meetings regularly to learn more about the trade and to network with other investors. It was at one of these local real estate meetings where we met Jeff for the first time.

We were teaching a class on year-end tax planning that night. On stage, we mostly talked about tax-minimization strategies to consider before the year ended. Over the course of an hour, we discussed such tactics as depreciation, accelerating tax write-offs, and shifting income to kids or legal entities. After our presentation, we stayed to answer any follow-up questions attendees had. During that time, Jeff approached us, introduced himself as a newbie investor, and asked for a fee quote for his tax returns that year.

After discovering that Jeff was single with a full-time job and no real estate investments, we felt that his tax return should be pretty straightforward. This is why we were shocked when Jeff told us that he had four companies that would also need tax returns filed.

Four companies? We couldn't imagine why someone with zero real estate properties would need four company tax returns filed. After speaking with Jeff further, we learned that he had hired a firm just a few weeks earlier to form these entities for him. This firm had advisors that formed entities for some of the most famous real estate investors in the United States.

Jeff believed he really did need all four of these entities. One of them was set up to hold his future rentals. The second one was for his plan to invest in tax liens. The third was for his note-buying business. Last but not least, the fourth entity was formed as a C corporation to help him with his tax deductions.

Now if you think this is too many entities, we are in total agreement with you. Our heart broke for Jeff when we heard that he had *spent over $10,000 in fees just to form these entities. "These attorneys are advisors to the real estate moguls you see on TV!" Jeff had excitedly proclaimed. "They have set up the best possible entity structures for me. Now, I haven't purchased any real estate or made any money yet, but I'm ready for that at any moment. In fact, I am flying out to New Orleans to attend a real estate flipping class next week. As soon as I return, I expect my business to start generating income. For now, I have a lot of expenses, and I am so glad that I set up my entities last week. Now I can write off all these classes and formation fees. What I need to know is how much will it cost for you to do my taxes for all my entities."*

If you consider yourself faint of heart, you probably want to stop reading here. The rest of this story is not pretty...

Don't Put the Cart Before the Horse

Jeff made a common mistake that we see newbie real estate investors make all the time—putting the cart before the horse. Essentially, he spent a large amount of money to form several legal entities when there was no real benefit for him:

- First, Jeff didn't have any real estate properties, so he didn't have liability concerns.
- Second, Jeff didn't have many personal assets, so he didn't need protection.
- Third, Jeff didn't have any business income to offset the real estate expenses.

Essentially, Jeff prematurely spent $10,000 in legal fees to form four specific entities when he should have invested his time and money into his first real estate deal instead. Jeff could have used that $10,000 as a down payment with a bank loan to purchase a small rental property worth $50,000. This property could have then provided him some good cash flow and appreciation. Also, once that property had been purchased, he could legitimately declare himself a property owner and real estate investor and could deduct his rental expenses.

Instead, Jeff's hard-earned money was spent on legal fees to form companies that, at that point, essentially served no purpose. Now that these entities had been formed, they had expenses of their own to operate and maintain, such as tax return costs, annual state fees, legal fees, and registered agent fees, just to name a few. We almost didn't have the heart to tell Jeff the truth, but we knew it was the right thing to do.

The first piece of advice we gave Jeff was to find the most affordable tax preparer he could and have that person prepare all his tax returns so he could be in compliance with the IRS. At this point, Jeff did not need to hire us and work with us on tax strategies. He could think about doing that once he started to earn money from his real estate ventures.

The second piece of advice we gave Jeff was to focus and take action. It sounded like Jeff was overeducated. There is a term—analysis paralysis—that refers to a situation in which a person has too much information and too many options, so much so that it actually prevents them from taking action. Jeff had taken so many classes on different real estate techniques that he never had time to actually refine and implement any single investment vehicle.

For Jeff, the financial downside of not taking action was apparent in the fact that he had slowly drained his savings over the past year and now had very little left to actually use for investing. The tax downside of not having any income was that it put hurdles on how much he could write off on his tax returns.

A Legal Entity Does Not Always Mean More Tax Deductions

Contrary to what Jeff's attorney had told him, forming a legal entity does not mean you are able to legitimately take tax deductions. You must still be able to prove that you have in fact started your business. Jeff had an uphill battle and faced a high audit risk if he were to take a tax deduction on his tax return while showing zero income for the year.

One of the biggest myths about legal entities is that you must have one to write off business expenses. Having a legal entity is not an IRS requirement to write off real estate or business expenses. On the contrary, the IRS simply requires that you have a "business," And business is defined as "activities with the goal of making profit."

For example, if you are a real estate agent and you operate under your personal name without any legal entities, you can still take most, if not all, of the same tax write-offs that a real estate agent with an LLC can take. Although certain entities can provide some special tax write-offs, the truth is that more than 90% of the common real estate–related write-offs can be taken whether you have a legal entity or not.

For example, if Jeff owned a rental property, he would be entitled to all the same tax write-offs for the following expenses, regardless of whether he held property in his personal name or in an LLC:

Jeff	Jeff's LLC
$9,600 Rental Income	$9,600 Rental Income
($2,600) Mortgage Interest	($2,600) Mortgage Interest
($780) Property Taxes	($780) Property Taxes
($425) Insurance Expense	($425) Insurance Expense
($950) Car and Travel Expense	($950) Car and Travel Expense
($645) Repair Costs	($645) Repair Costs
($350) Education and Seminars	($350) Education and Seminars
($200) Real Estate License Fees	($200) Real Estate License Fees
($200) Telephone Expenses	($200) Telephone Expenses
($470) Meals and Entertainment	($470) Meals and Entertainment
($1,300) Depreciation	($1,300) Depreciation
$1,680 Net Taxable Income	$1,680 Net Taxable Income

As you can see, forming a legal entity does not necessarily mean that you are eligible for more of a tax deduction. Also, many people don't know that in the eyes of the IRS, real estate– and business-related expenses may be deductible regardless of where they are paid from.

Moving Money Between You and Your Business

What if you already have an entity formed, and there is not enough income in that entity to pay for certain expenses? For example, perhaps you have a rental property in an LLC that is cash flow negative because a tenant moved out. You would need to list the property for rent again and may have to pay out of your own pocket for marketing expenses if there isn't enough cash in the LLC bank account. This doesn't create a problem for tax purposes as long as it's documented. Simply keep any out-of-pocket expense receipts in your company folder, and once your company is out of the red, write a check to reimburse yourself for the costs that you incurred during the income lull.

It is important to note that we don't recommend doing this very often, because you want to keep personal and business money separate; otherwise, this could affect your asset and audit protection. However, if you do accidentally use personal money to pay for a business expense, simply have the company reimburse you for that cost. This is a way to personally receive tax-free money from the business, while also creating tax deductions.

So with regard to creating entity structures, don't put the cart before the horse. Make sure that you have real estate–related income before spending a ton of cash to form your legal entities. After all, our goal as investors is to make money in real estate, right? The earlier we start making money, the better, so keeping our focus on income is key.

What Does All This Mean?

Before you form an entity for your real estate business, have a discussion with your personal tax and legal advisors. Given that each investor has different financials, goals, and strategies, the best type of legal entity for one investor may not be so great for the next. Although it is easy to get excited about a new investing venture, make sure your advisory team helps you put a plan in place before you spend money on legal entity formation.

Don't forget, you can claim most business expense tax deductions whether you have a legal entity or not. Expenses paid personally may be tax deductible as long as they are business related. Simply having an entity does not necessarily mean you have a legitimate business to write off your expenses. Showing income is key to deducting a certain expense on your tax return. And after all, isn't our goal as real estate investors to generate as much income as possible as quickly as possible?

One Size Does Not Fit All

A lawyer to an asset protection specialist is like a doctor to a heart surgeon. In any event, would you ever cut open your own chest?

–Scott Smith, Attorney

Ever have trouble sleeping at night? If so, you must have seen some of those late-night infomercials:

"Call right now, and you can have not one, not two, not three, but four WizzyWidgets for just $19.95! But you must call now, because this offer will only last for the next ten minutes."

You may not have actually needed a WizzyWidget (and you don't even know what a WizzyWidget is, because we just made it up), but this deal just sounds too good to pass up. But as you read the tiny fine print on the screen, you notice that each of the four WizzyWidgets costs an additional $29.95 in shipping and handling fees. So rather than paying only $19.95, as the commercial would have you think, you're paying $19.95 plus almost $120 in shipping and handling fees.

Typically, if someone says, "You must buy this now" or "This deal won't be around after today," there is a high likelihood that you are being ripped off. The "buy now" tactic distracts people from their rational side. They become so afraid of missing out on a good deal that they just pay up without doing the necessary research.

So what does this have to do with real estate investing? Well, scams just like those late-night infomercials exist in the real estate world as well. Most people encounter this tactic on TV or at those kiosks in the mall, but they are actually big business in the real estate world. If you have ever attended a large-scale real estate conference or seminar, you have probably seen some in action.

One of the most commonly seen "buy now" gimmicks in real estate actually happens with entity formation. So-called entity experts set up shop at real estate conferences or hold seminars to scare the heck out of investors with horror stories about people who have lost everything because of lawsuits. The solution, they will tell you, is creating the right entities to hold your real estate assets. Now don't get us wrong, entity structuring is a very important component of real estate investing. Setting up your entities correctly can help you both protect your assets and minimize taxes. However, what we especially dislike about these "buy now" entity companies is that most of them follow a one-size-fits-all mentality. And as with everything else in the real estate world, there is no one-size-fits-all answer. The right type of entity for you and your investments can differ drastically from what would be best for the person sitting next to you.

Very often, the entity formation companies will target new investors who have only a few properties or perhaps no properties yet. They will typically tell you about some sort of "ironclad" structure that is guaranteed to get you the best asset protection and help you avoid taxes. Very often, we have seen clients who have set up multiple entities in states such as Nevada or Wyoming. While creating entities in these states may seem like a no-brainer, considering that neither one has income taxes, doing so could actually be disastrous with regard to fees, maintenance, and taxes if you don't plan correctly.

> ***Real Life:*** *Connie went to one of these entity creation seminars years ago and lived to tell about it. Connie was scared straight by the presenter's story of one property owner who lost his life savings to a tenant who claimed a crack in the stairs in front of the house caused him to fall and break his arm. After that story, Connie was sure she was overexposed and needed to update her entities right away. Connie was a client of ours who lived in California. She owned two rental properties and at the time owned both of them under one LLC.*
>
> *After the seminar, Connie felt that she needed more. After all, she certainly did not want to end up like the man in the story who*

had worked so hard and lost everything to one overzealous tenant.

Also, what the entity expert had offered at the seminar sounded like a great deal. For just $3,000, Connie could get four legal entities plus federal Employer Identification Numbers (EINs) for each entity. This was the "ironclad" entity structure that was supposed to provide Connie the best protection and included the following:

- *Asset protection by having one LLC for each property*
- *A holding company to own the other LLCs*
- *Tax savings by forming entities in Nevada, which has no income tax*
- *A management entity to help Connie with maximizing her tax deductions*

As the crowd of real estate investors flocked to the back of the room, Connie was very tempted to join them. Thankfully, something inside her told her to take a step back and rethink the structure. She recalled speaking to us about entities previously but couldn't quite remember why we suggested not setting up multiple entities. She made the decision to speak with us about the structuring strategy she'd learned about at the conference before pulling the trigger. After one of the sales people from the entity formation company promised to follow up with her in a few days to help her set up her entities, Connie bravely walked away from the sale and gave us a call the first thing the next morning.

So did Connie make the right decision by not taking advantage of the one-size-fits-all entity structure? Let's find out.

The deal Connie was offered seemed almost too good to be true, with asset protection, more tax write-offs, and no income taxes. According to the entity expert, the $3,000 total package price was a steal, because normally, each entity alone would cost about $3,000. However, this discounted package came with strings attached. The offer was a "buy now" tactic, so the discounted price wouldn't last long. In fact, the price was good for that day only. After the seminar, the $3,000 bundle deal would disappear, and prices would return to $3,000 per entity.

As you may have guessed, this "ironclad" entity structure was a one-size-fits-all approach, so according to the salesman, it didn't matter where you invested, what type of investments you were making, or even how much money was being made, this structure would give you exactly what you needed.

The Real Cost

Remember how the entity expert claimed that Nevada was a great state to form the entities in, because it has no income tax? Well, although it is true that Nevada has no state income tax (which is great if you live there), simply forming an entity in Nevada does not mean that you are exempt from paying income taxes in your home state if you live elsewhere. This is a common misconception that investors are led to believe.

Take Connie's situation, for example. Because she lives in California, she would still be required to pay taxes on the rental income she earned through her Nevada entity as a California resident. So even though Connie wouldn't need to pay income taxes in Nevada, she would not save California taxes. Plus, with new entities, she would be required to pay some additional fees as well.

Fees for the State of Formation

Once an entity has been formed, all the other costs start to add up. For example, if Connie had formed these Nevada entities, she probably would have needed a registered agent in Nevada. That costs about $75 per entity per year, for a total of $300 for registered agent fees. Someone needs to maintain the entities, with meetings and minutes and all the other entity formalities, and of course, the entity formation company can provide this service for Connie for just $150 per entity per year, adding up to $600. Nevada also has an annual filing fee of $75 for each entity formed in the state, totaling $300 for all four. In addition, Nevada requires business owners to file an annual list of managers, which has a $125 fee, and this is on top of the $200 business license fee. These forms add an additional $1,300 annually for each entity.

Fees for the State of the Owner's Residency

What about the state fees in the state where the investor lives? In Connie's example, because she was a California resident, the state of California would require her to register her Nevada entities in California. This is not a small cost, given that each entity in California is subject to a minimum fee of

$800 each year. Again, this is just the minimum fee. This means that even if Connie had no income for the year, each of her Nevada entities must still pay California the $800 fee per year. This would be an annual cost of $3,200 in fees for the state of California alone.

Fees for the State Where the Properties Are Located

If the investment property is in yet a different state, there may be additional fees or taxes on that. Connie's properties were located in Tennessee, and Tennessee is one state where LLCs are subject to both a franchise tax and an excise tax. So, depending on the value of the properties, this could mean an additional $400 in state fees.

But it doesn't end there. What about tax returns? Each year, the entities may be required to file tax returns with the IRS and the state, depending on who the owners are, where they live, and where the properties are located. To be conservative, let's assume another $600 or so each year to pay a CPA to file tax returns for each entity.

There is a misconception that if you form an entity but don't use it during the year, no tax returns must be filed. Although sometimes an entity owned by a single person may not be required to file a tax return, there are instances where that entity may still need to file a tax return each year. In fact, if you have an entity that is owned by more than one person, the LLC is likely required to file an annual tax return with the IRS and the state, even if this entity never earned any income.

Let's break down what Connie would have actually been facing in terms of total costs had she taken advantage of this $3,000 one-size-fits-all entity package:

Annual Fee Breakdown		
Nevada Annual List of Managers Fee	$125 x 4	$500
Nevada Annual Business License Fee	$200 x 4	$800
Nevada Annual Registered Agent Fee	$75 x 4	$300
Nevada Annual Filing Fees	$75 x 4	$300
California Fees	$800 x 4	$3,200
Tennessee Fees	$100 x 4	$400
Entity Maintenance Fees	$150 x 4	$600
Tax Return Filing Fees	$600 x 4	$2,400
Total Annual Cost		$8,500

Connie's $3,000 bundle would have actually been closer to an $11,500 bundle.

It just didn't make sense for Connie to use this supposedly "ironclad" structure. She had very little equity in one of her rentals and was actually underwater on the second. It would not have been prudent for her to spend $3,000 to form these entities and then spend $8,500 each year to protect what little equity she did have in the rentals.

In fact, the $8,500 in entity maintenance costs would have just about wiped out the net cash flow she made each year from the rentals themselves! With so little equity in her rentals, it was perfectly sufficient for her to have just one LLC to hold her two properties. This one LLC was in place, after all, to protect her personal assets from potential tenant lawsuits, according to her asset protection attorney.

On the tax side, Connie was able to write off all the same expenses using one LLC as she would have if she had formed all those other holding and management entities. Had she opted for the bundled package, she would not have benefited from any more write-offs than she already did.

This is just one example of how costly a one-size-fits-all entity solution can be for real estate investors. Each investor has their own financial, tax, and property profile, and each of these profiles helps determine what type of entity or entities would be best for that investor. As with anything else in real estate, you must consider any options from a cost-benefit standpoint before making any big decisions. Although the entity expert's four-entity plan may have been a bad idea for Connie, it could be the ideal structure for a different investor. This is why it is extremely important to meet regularly with your tax and legal advisors throughout the year to ensure that your entity structure is sufficient for what you are currently doing and what you plan to do.

Had Connie joined the other seminar attendees at the back of the room and formed the four proposed entities, we may have later advised her to dissolve them. And if you think the entity structure firm would dissolve an entity free of charge, think again. Companies typically charge several hundred dollars to help people dissolve an entity—and this is after the investor has paid thousands of dollars to set up their entities in the first place. Without the right information and advice, Connie could have spent thousands of dollars on services, taxes, and fees to create and then shut down entities she never needed in the first place.

What Does All This Mean?

Ask any savvy investor, and they will tell you that real estate investing is just like any other business. You should take the time necessary to fully understand what costs you are incurring and what benefits you will receive before spending your money. There are plenty of scammers in the real estate world, just as there are in other business areas. There is the saying "Free advice is worth what you pay for it." We're not saying that you can't ever learn something useful from free advice, but rather that you should always consult with your advisors on such complex and permanent decisions as entity structuring.

Just as with shoes, there is no one-size-fits-all solution with entity structuring. Before forming any entity, be sure you understand what the annual maintenance costs will be each year. Take a cost-benefit view to determine which type of entity and how many make sense for your real estate portfolio. Before you pull the trigger, meet with your personal advisor to discuss where you invest, what you invest in, and how much profit you make so they can help you to develop the best entity structures for your specific situation.

Remember, the next time you hear someone—anyone—tell you they have a one-size-fits-all entity solution for you, make sure to run quickly… out the door!

How to Wake Up from Your Bookkeeping Nightmare

Make sure you file your tax return on time! And remember that, even though income taxes can be a "pain in the neck," the folks at the IRS are regular people just like you, except that they can destroy your life.

– Dave Barry

In our years working with real estate investors all over the United States, we have yet to meet anyone who said they enjoy bookkeeping. No one gets excited about spending the afternoon or a weekend going over numbers and receipts for their real estate activities. And when we say no one, we mean no one—not even the two of us.

However, bookkeeping does play a very important role in investing. Ever heard the saying "What gets measured gets managed"? This applies to all sorts of businesses; real estate is no exception. If you are a landlord, how do you know how well your rental is performing if you do not have accurate income and expense data? If you are doing a fix and flip, how do you know whether your project is within budget and on track to make a profit if you don't know where you stand? In addition to preventing you from effectively managing your real estate, a lack of bookkeeping can sometimes create other problems for investors, especially at tax time.

Real Life: *"Your wages have been garnished." Rather than looking at his paycheck amount that month, Steve was staring at these words on the piece of paper in front of him. It was unfathomable to him that he owed more than $17,000 in income taxes to the IRS.*

Steve was no dummy. He was well aware that he had not filed taxes in a few years, but he did not expect that it would come to this. He knew other people who had gotten their wages garnished by the IRS, but never in a million years did he think he would be one of them. In fact, only a few years earlier, Steve would have looked down on those people who did not file their annual taxes, especially because he always filed his returns as early as possible. After all, when life was simple, taxes were easy. That was before Steve started investing in real estate.

Things changed three years ago, when Steve met up with an old friend he'd served with in the navy. He learned from his friend that real estate was a great asset in which to invest. Steve found the idea of getting monthly cash flow appealing and saw the benefits of building wealth through appreciation.

With his friend's help, Steve started investing in real estate. Before long, he had purchased three rental properties in his hometown. He was happy with his investment decisions, because cash flow was good, and for the most part, he had really great tenants.

Unfortunately, his problems began when he attempted to do his tax returns that year. After installing the tax software, Steve quickly realized that he had bitten off more than he could chew. The software asked him all sorts of questions that he was not sure how to answer. To top it all off, TurboTax asked Steve for the dollar amount of some rental expenses that he honestly did not know. Initially, he pulled together the monthly statements from his two bank accounts and three credit cards, in hopes of getting organized. He would start looking through the bank statements and tiny receipts to make sense of it all, but then he would conveniently find something else more pressing to do and abandon the pile of papers.

With everything else on Steve's plate those days, bookkeeping definitely was nowhere near the top of his to-do list. Like most investors, he did not really care for the task, because he found it tedious and boring. I think most of us can agree that bookkeeping is certainly not the most exciting part of being an investor. In fact, Steve would unconsciously (and probably consciously, too!) try to do whatever he could to avoid doing his books. Every time he saw the calendar reminder pop up on his phone to work on the bookkeeping for his rentals, he would try to think of anything else he needed to do that was "more important," whether it was calling the bank on a refinance or searching for new investment properties. Of course, without the financial information for his rental properties, Steve was not able to finish his personal tax returns.

Weeks went by before he finally abandoned the task completely. Those weeks turned into months, and the months turned into years, as Steve's pile of receipts gathered more and more dust. Only when he received the notice about the IRS garnishing his wages did he decide it was time to hunker down, get his books in order, and file his returns.

When we met with Steve the first time, he was both scared and overwhelmed. The IRS was ruthless about wage garnishment. Losing a large portion of his paycheck each month was a huge problem for Steve, as it would be for most people, and something clearly had to be done quickly to get him caught up with his taxes.

When Steve originally purchased QuickBooks Pro software, he had intended to go backward in time to enter each and every bank transaction for the previous three years. This was a daunting task, and the added stress was simply too much for Steve. He was very clear during our first meeting that he was prepared to spend a ton of time and money to have us assist him in getting it all done.

That is why Steve was pleasantly surprised when we told him that we knew a shortcut that would get his bookkeeping caught up. In fact, he really didn't need to enter every single transaction from the past three years into his QuickBooks.

The most efficient way to get his books up-to-date was "quick and dirty bookkeeping."

Quick & Dirty Bookkeeping

Getting the Correct Income Amounts

To be clear, quick and dirty bookkeeping is neither a brand new software nor a traditional accounting methodology. This is simply what we call the quickest way to catch up on one's bookkeeping to get to an end result. The first step in Steve's case was to request an IRS transcript indicating how much income had been reported to the IRS for Steve each year.

By filling out a one-page Form 4506-T, Steve was easily able to request tax transcripts for all three years that were overdue. Once the IRS received this form, they mailed an account transcript showing what other people had reported under Steve's name as income each year. For example, the amount of money his property management company collected was on this transcript, as were certain other items, such as mortgage interest paid to the bank.

Essentially, getting a copy of this tax transcript helped Steve ensure that his records matched what others had reported to the IRS. This is a quick and easy way to arrive at the main income amount without going through the bank statements in detail. The best part, believe it or not, is that the IRS will send you the transcript for free.

Getting the Correct Expense Amounts

Many major expenses can also be obtained without having to go through every bank and credit card transaction. For investors in rental real estate like Steve, some of the common large expenses include mortgage interest, insurance, points, and property taxes. Simply contact the mortgage company to request a year-end 1098 Form, and this document will generally show the total annual mortgage interest, taxes, points, and insurance paid.

Other Key Rental Expenses

Using the two tricks we've just described, you can generally capture a few of the largest key items that relate to the income and expenses of your rental property.

With most of the big items now out of the way, we worked with Steve to identify some other common expenses we typically see for rental properties. Steve indicated that although he was making small repairs from time to time, he recalled two major repairs he had done on two of his rentals during the previous three years. To ensure that he captured both of those repairs as deductions on his tax returns, the easiest thing for Steve to do was think back to the months in which the expenses incurred and then look through those months' bank and credit card statements to identify what those larger amounts were.

When time is of the essence, we suggest this quick and dirty bookkeeping method to ensure that you capture the larger expense items. If you bought a laptop that was used in your real estate business, look that purchase up in your bank statements. If you purchased a new car two years ago that was used for the business, make sure you take that into account. When you are trying to meet an IRS deadline for a late tax return and garnishment or liens are involved, skip the little things and focus on the expense items that will affect your return the most. This approach can help you get caught up and in compliance sooner.

Leverage Your Time with the Right Bookkeeping Software

To be clear, quick and dirty bookkeeping is never recommended for people who are not in serious trouble with the IRS and facing tax liens. It is only for the direst of situations, when you must produce the most accurate information in a short amount of time.

In fact, for most investors, QuickBooks Pro is a wonderful software program. Not only is it easy to use, but it also has automation tools and powerful reporting capabilities that can meet the needs of some of the largest real estate investors around.

As we helped Steve catch up on his past due tax returns, we also helped him set up his QuickBooks so he could enter everything correctly going forward.

Ease of Use

There are many different types of software available at different price points and with different capabilities, but what we love about QuickBooks Pro is that it is very user friendly. In fact, when you set up the books within the software, it actually has a built-in chart of accounts especially for real estate investors. This chart of accounts is a template that includes common accounts that an investor would use on a day-to-day basis, such as rental income, security deposits, management fees, mortgage insurance, and property taxes.

Simply indicate in the software that you are in the rental real estate business, and the system automatically creates the entire chart of accounts for you. Not only does this save time—especially for those who are new to bookkeeping, like Steve—but the chart of accounts can also help new investors avoid mistakes often made by creating incorrect account names. Because different accounts can have significantly different tax treatments, it is important to make sure that the accounts are named and used correctly.

Security Deposits Versus Rental Income

For example, many investors do not know that security deposits and rental income are treated differently on a tax return. Security deposits are payments that you hold on to until the tenant moves out. Because this is money that you may be required to return to the tenant, this is not income for you in the year you receive it. If a new investor did not know that security deposits and rents have different tax treatments, they may make the mistake of classifying both these items as income and thus accidentally overpay in taxes. With two accounts in the QuickBooks chart of accounts that show Rental Income versus Security Deposits, the investor can more easily book the correct transaction and thereby minimize the likelihood of an error.

Automation

One of the main reasons Steve, like many investors, dreaded bookkeeping was that he just did not have the time to do it. Steve had a full-time job and a wife and kids to take care of, so the last thing on his mind at the end of the week was getting in front of the computer and spending countless hours poring over bank statements and receipts.

To help overcome this issue and significantly reduce the time he needed each month to keep his books up-to-date, Steve linked his bank account and credit card account with QuickBooks. This way, he was able to automatically transfer large chunks of information from the bank directly to his QuickBooks software with just the click of a button. Rather than Steve having to enter the date, payee, amount, description, and account related to each transaction, close to 90% of the bookkeeping work was now automated, thanks to the online sync function within QuickBooks.

Once the automation was set up, all Steve needed to do each month was review the downloaded transactions in QuickBooks and indicate what type of expense account each one related to (i.e., repairs, mortgage interest, property taxes, etc.). The QuickBooks automation function not only significantly decreases the time needed to enter data from the bank, but it also minimize input errors. This tool, if used correctly, can help investors like Steve cut their monthly bookkeeping time by close to two-thirds.

In the end, Steve decided to hand his books over to us going forward. He deemed us his "accountants" for his real estate business and signed us on as part of his team. He was more than happy to hand this part of his investing business over to the professionals, because he had never really liked it anyway. As he left our office, that nagging little voice in the back of his mind was finally gone. He had washed his hands of the bookkeeping and tax-filing part of his business, along with all his built-up stress and worry.

Powerful Reporting

Another advantage QuickBooks offers for real estate is its powerful reporting capabilities. Now you may be asking, "Reporting capabilities? Don't I just enter the numbers into the software, and it's all done?"

The answer is no; simply entering the data into QuickBooks is not all there is to bookkeeping. In fact, what comes after the information has been entered is the most important part.

Review the Financial Statement Reports

Once the information has been entered, you as the business owner will want to print the software reports to review. The software is designed to run all the common financial statement reports, including profit and loss statements, balance sheets, and cash flow statements. It is extremely important for you to review each of these reports every month.

QuickBooks allows you to organize your financials by property. This is highly recommended for investors who own multiple properties. Organizing your books by property allows you to run profit and loss reports separately, which can show you how well each rental is doing. On the other hand, if one of your rentals has incurred significant expenses, reviewing the profit and loss report each month can help you easily identify the issue and determine ways to resolve it.

Reviewing your financial statements monthly is even more important if you are undertaking a large repair or improvement project on a property. To keep within your budget, you should keep detailed records of your expenses. When evaluating which repairs are reasonable enough to undertake, look at the numbers before committing to any huge repair or improvement project. And when you are in the process of a big improvement project, make sure to keep track of your financial progress as frequently as possible. This way you can always be up-to-date on how much has been spent on the project. By identifying which improvements could cause you to go over budget, you can keep an eye out for any necessary adjustments that need to be made.

In other words, reviewing your financial statements monthly can help you identify problems before things get out of hand. Checking over the financial reports QuickBooks generates can often help you identify errors as well. For example, if you know that last month, your net rental income was roughly $1,000, but the QuickBooks report shows a net loss of $3,000, you know something was entered incorrectly and can dig into your records to identify where that error occurred. Going over your reports helps you capture mistakes and allows you to make timely decisions.

Separate Bank Accounts

Whether you have a separate legal entity or not, one of the easiest ways to save a ton of time and headache with your bookkeeping is to have separate bank and credit card accounts for your real estate and personal items. Remember how hard it was for Steve to go back through his bank statements from previous years and recall which expenses were for his rentals and which were personal? Well, this problem can be avoided simply by setting up different accounts, so that you use one for real estate and a separate one for personal items.

If you have an LLC or any other type of business entity, you definitely need to open a bank account in that entity's name. In Steve's case, even though he did not have another entity to own his real estate, he could still set up a different bank account and use that exclusively for his rental income and expenses. This way, he would be able to clearly separate his investing transactions from his personal items at bookkeeping time. It would also be much easier for him to be confident that everything that went through that second account relates to his real estate investments.

Don't Forget to Reconcile to Your Bank Statements

A common bookkeeping mistake we see investors and bookkeepers make is failing to reconcile bank statements. So what exactly is reconciling? It's is a way to double-check your documents against the information the bank has. For example, if you wrote a check for your mortgage payment this month, but it had not been cashed by the mortgage company yet, the bank would not have a record of the transaction. This is something you would definitely want to keep an eye on, in case it is never cashed. Perhaps the mortgage company never received it. In that case, you should follow up and investigate.

Another example of a reconciling item is a bank or service fee. Most of the time, people are not aware of each fee associated with their account, and the bank generally takes these fees straight from people's account without sending an invoice or notice. The fees are usually only broken down on the bank statement. Once you receive your bank statement, you would be able to record in your books any fees that were charged that month. With most accounting software, such as QuickBooks, reconciling your accounts each month is a simple and fairly automated process.

Are Property Management Reports Enough?

If you have a property management company that oversees your rentals, it may send you management reports each month. A question we commonly get is whether these property management reports are sufficient, and if they make bookkeeping unnecessary.

The answer to this question depends on your property and how you operate your business. We had a client who owned a small piece of commercial property directly across the street from a hospital. He knew that the property made good money and was concerned about owing a lot of taxes on the $12,000 net profit shown on his property management reports each month. Based on those numbers, he was anticipating close to $144,000 of net income for the year from that commercial property.

However, when we worked with him on his tax planning, we noticed that his property management report was missing a few key items. For example, the management report did not include mortgage interest, property taxes, or insurance. All three of these expenses were paid directly by our client, so the property manager had never even seen these statements.

After factoring in all these additional expenses, the net profit was really only $4,000 each month—not nearly as high as the owner initially thought.

In addition, rental property owners can often incur out-of-pocket expenses related to the property. These out-of-pocket expenses are also generally not included on a property management report, as the managers typically are not aware of them. Although property management reports do provide a good starting place for bookkeeping, you still need to make sure you understand what is and is not included in the report so you can calculate the true profit and loss on your rental.

Cash Flow Management

One of the most crucial areas for real estate investors is cash flow. Accurate bookkeeping allows you to have more control over your finances. As such, the more often you monitor your cash flow, the better.

Managing and reviewing your books monthly is better than doing so quarterly. However, reviewing them quarterly is still better than doing it just once a year. The more frequently you do your bookkeeping, the simpler the process is, because recalling what you did last month is much easier than recalling what you did six months ago. Also, updating and reviewing your books more frequently gives you more control over your finances.

Analyzing your cash flow on a regular basis will help you determine whether your money is being used in the best way possible for your property. A correctly designed and executed bookkeeping system will let you monitor how your cash flow fluctuates throughout the year. This in turn enables you to make informed and timely decisions about your investment properties.

Don't Forget to Reimburse Yourself

No matter how organized you are, there are bound to be times when you inadvertently use personal money to pay for real estate–related expenses. During your grocery trip to Costco, for example, you may remember that you need some copy paper or pens for the office. Or while mailing your holiday cards, you may realize you need more postage for your real estate mailers. If you do not have your company card with you, it is okay to pay for these expenses with cash or your personal card. Just make sure to reimburse yourself from the business account later to keep the expenses within the correct account.

We do not recommend that you do this often, of course. Ideally, you'll pay for real estate expenses with business funds and personal expenses with personal funds. In those certain unexpected cases when you pay business expenses with personal funds, here are a two ways to ensure that you capture these costs for your bookkeeping and tax deductions.

Petty Cash

Consider keeping a drawer or box of petty cash for minor day-to-day expenses. For example, if you have a petty cash box with $300, you can dip into it when you need to order lunch for your contractors or to buy that $25 gift card for your landscaper. Just remember to keep these receipts and record the expenses in QuickBooks.

Reimbursements

For larger amounts, simply keep a copy of the receipt for the money you spent and then have the business account reimburse you. So if you spent $50 on paper and pens at Costco, simply have the business account write a $50 check to you personally. This way, you can record a $50 office supplies expense in QuickBooks to capture the write-off.

Do What Works for You

Remember, QuickBooks may or may not be the best solution for your particular business activities. It depends largely on how much time you are able to dedicate to bookkeeping and how comfortable you are with learning software.

Hiring a bookkeeper or a CPA may or may not be the best solution, either. This depends on the complexity of your investments as well as on your resources in terms of budget and time. Unless you have accounting experience, it may make sense to hire a professional to at least help you set your books up correctly. Once that has been done, you can either do the bookkeeping yourself, or if you value your time, consider hiring the best you can afford.

Bookkeeping doesn't need to be hard or tedious, and it doesn't need to be done by a CPA or computer software. It does, however, need to work for you. So whether you use QuickBooks or Excel, or you hand the job over to someone else entirely, make sure bookkeeping is built into your investing system so you can enjoy the benefits of having more control over your money and investments.

So what happened to Steve's wage garnishment? Well, it turned out that the $17,000 in back taxes was all due to the gross rents the property management company had reported to the IRS. Because Steve hadn't filed tax returns originally, the IRS assumed that he had no expenses to offset the rental income and assessed him taxes and penalties based on that income.

After filing the overdue tax returns, which included all the mortgage interest, taxes, depreciation, and other write-offs, Steve ended up with an overall tax loss and did not have to pay any taxes on the rental income he earned during those previous years.

After that horrific experience and now armed with a more efficient way of doing his monthly bookkeeping, Steve will be one of the first in line to file his taxes each year.

What Does All This Mean?

A question investors often ask us is "What bookkeeping solution is best for real estate investors?" As you may have guessed, the answer is that it depends! The most effective way to do bookkeeping is whatever works best for you. Your ability and willingness to keep your books up-to-date is the single most important element of effective bookkeeping. Having the most powerful software sitting on your shelf the entire year still in the shrink-wrap will not help you with your bookkeeping. Having a bookkeeper that you constantly avoid will not help with your books, either. Use whatever method works best for you and your investments, whether that's software, Excel, an outside bookkeeper, or even just plain old pen and paper.

More importantly, be sure to review your financials frequently to identify how your investments are performing and to gain better control over your cash flow.

RETIREMENT PLANNING

Taking Control of Your Retirement Money

Wide diversification is only required when investors do not understand what they are doing.

– Warren Buffett

There is a widely held belief that diversification is the key to effective investing. You often hear advisors reference sayings such as "Don't put all your eggs in one basket." However, we believe that this type of diversification philosophy may be flawed. After all, wouldn't investing in something that we know and understand produce better results than investing in something we don't? If we understand real estate better than automobile manufacturing, for example, wouldn't we be able to create better returns by investing in real estate in areas we are familiar with?

> ***Real Life:*** *As always, Roger was dreading dinner with his folks. He always felt so anxious meeting with them, because every dinner went the same way. His parents would start with small talk about current events, weather, and the new neighbors they weren't too fond of. As soon as the entrees would arrive and Roger was trapped, his parents would jump headfirst into the topics of money and his job. Then dessert course would come with a full-blown argument and a lecture from his father. It was an unchanging pattern, and Roger knew this*

dinner would be just like all the others.

Roger's father had worked his entire life in the financial services industry as an actuarial. Roger and his dad had butted heads a few years earlier, when Roger quit his corporate job as an engineer to become a full-time real estate investor. According to his dad, Roger was making the biggest mistake of his life by leaving the comfort and safety of a steady paycheck to follow a foolish dream of becoming the next real estate guru.

However, Roger was confident in his dream. He wanted to accomplish more in life than his parents had. Roger's plan to get licensed in real estate and earn a living by selling properties and acquiring rentals was working out pretty close to what he had been hoping for. In just three years, Roger had almost replaced his corporate pay with his real estate agent commissions and the cash flow from his duplex. The local real estate market was depressed, and Roger quickly learned that this was actually good news for his investment plans. Generally when prices are low, cash flow can be high for rentals. With more inventory on the market than buyers, Roger could potentially snatch up a few properties with less cash and build up his rental portfolio faster.

Last year was a good year on the retail side for Roger as well. In meeting with his tax advisor, Roger learned that he had made about $90,000 in net profits from his real estate agent commissions. This was his highest income yet since leaving his engineering job, which was good news. The bad news was that he might need to pay close to $30,000 in income taxes to the IRS and the state. Roger had known that he would have to pay some taxes, he just didn't expect them to equal almost one-third of his net income

During his year-end tax planning meeting, we introduced Roger to the power of retirement account planning. We told him that as long as his retirement account was open by year-end, he could wait until the following year to make contributions and take tax deductions. So, Roger went ahead and opened the account but held off on making any retirement contributions. He wanted to wait and see what his taxes owed were before making a decision about contributing to the retirement account.

The Best of All Three Worlds

Roger really wanted to keep his cash to invest in real estate rather than putting it into an account to sit for most of his life. His present goal was to acquire as many rentals as possible in the depressed market while business was good, and he felt that putting money into a retirement account meant less money to use for purchasing rentals. After meeting with us, he realized that his worries were largely unfounded. Roger learned that he could put money into his new 401(k) plan, take a tax write-off, and then use that money to invest in real estate. In fact, if he used this strategy correctly, the rental income he generated within the retirement account could grow tax deferred for years and years. It would be taxed only when Roger withdrew the earnings at his retirement.

This caught Roger's attention. He didn't realize that he could do so many things with a retirement account:

- Put money into an account to reduce current taxes

- Use that retirement money for real estate investing

- Benefit from tax-deferred growth on the money in the account

Roger was excited to learn that all this was indeed possible. For Roger, the best way to do this was to put $40,000 into his 401(k) plan to start. He could then take a $40,000 tax deduction, which would save him close to $13,000 in taxes he would have otherwise paid to the government. Instead, he had $40,000 in his retirement account that he could use to purchase a rental property. He could then let that property grow tax deferred over the next three decades.

To Roger, this was a dream come true: something to help him both save on taxes and invest in even more real estate. He wondered why he had never heard of this "self-directed investing" strategy before. Roger had never heard it mentioned on the news or read about it in any magazine. At any rate, he was happy that he now had a potential solution to his tax problems.

Although Roger's dinners with his parents usually ended in an argument, he thought he should maybe run this idea by his father to get his input and feedback. His dad did work for a financial planner, after all, and he knew quite a bit about retirement accounts. However, Roger's dad was extremely upset by the idea of Roger opening a self-directed retirement account. His dad failed to see the benefit of using retirement money for real estate investing. In fact, he questioned whether the strategy was even legal, given that he had never heard of it before in all his years working in the financial sector.

Diversification Versus Specialization

The concept of self-directed investing is actually allowed by the IRS. Although the code does not specify what you are allowed to invest in, IRS Publication 590 discusses what types of transactions are not allowed (e.g., investing in life insurance). The concept of self-directed investing is not new. In fact, it has been around since the tax code was revised in 1986. So for almost thirty years, the IRS has allowed people to invest their retirement money in assets other than stocks, bonds, and mutual funds. This was reaffirmed in the court case Swanson V. Commissioner 106 T.C. 76 (1996), in which the IRS confirmed that IRA-owned LLCs could participate in self-directed investing. This landmark case helped clarify that even the IRS views self-directed investments as perfectly legal. The reason so few people know about this opportunity is simply lack of education.

Self-directed investing, Roger learned, was the same as using regular investment vehicles, such as IRAs, Roth IRAs, and 401(k)s. The same benefits apply for self-directed accounts. You put money into the retirement account to get either a current-year tax write-off and tax deferred growth or to get permanently tax-free money. The only difference between the traditional retirement vehicles and self-directed retirement vehicles is what you can invest in.

Traditional retirement accounts limit you to the investment funds presented by the investment firm. These can include all types of stocks, bonds, and mutual funds. A self-directed retirement account, on the other hand, lets you choose what you want to invest in.

- If you wanted to use your retirement money to buy a property down the street, you can.

- If you wanted to lend some of your retirement money to a friend for their business, you can.

- If your cousin started a software company that is about to take off, and you wanted to use your retirement money to invest in that business, you can.

The Conspiracy Theory

So why don't more people know about self-directed investing?

The ugly truth is that because most financial planners are compensated based on investments made in the stock market, there has not been much incentive to inform or advise clients on how to use retirement funds for real estate and other self-directed alternative assets. Not until recently has public education and awareness grown about self-directed investing strategies. Those who are using the strategy today are considered ahead of the trend.

Roger's dad wasn't buying the idea, so they ended dinner, once again, on a bad note. He knew, though, that his dad would do some research now that he had brought up the self-directed IRA strategy. Sure enough, Roger's dad reluctantly looked up the IRS regulations, and at their next family dinner, he admitted that he had to agree with Roger. He had done his research, and this indeed was a legitimate strategy allowed by the IRS and not some wacky or illegal concept sold in a back alley.

If you think Roger's dad was about to give up, though, you are dead wrong. Instead, he brought up the issue of diversification. Seeing that Roger already had almost all his cash invested in a duplex rental property, wouldn't it make sense to invest the retirement money in the stock market? After all, we all know that diversification minimizes risk, right?

Although diversification may be a great way to reduce risk for some, it can be terrible for others. Let's take Roger, for example. Roger does not understand a thing about the stock market. In fact, he can't really tell you the difference between a large cap stock and a small cap stock. Roger has never read any financial reports of public companies and does not know who makes decisions on shareholder dividends or how they are paid out.

Real estate, on the other hand, is something Roger knows a lot about. He knows what market rent is between various local neighborhoods. He knows when site plans are proposed and when large national retailers are ready to build. He knows how much properties are selling for and more importantly, what people are buying them for. These are Roger's unique advantages. Real estate is his expertise; it's what he does day in and day out. He could exert more control over real estate deals than he ever could by owning a share of Coca-Cola stock. In fact, with the right recipe, Roger might generate much higher returns by putting his money in real estate rather than the stock market. For Roger, there really isn't any benefit to diversifying his retirement money into the stock market, so it's probably safer for him to invest that money in real estate.

Once Roger explained this, his dad finally seemed to understand and to agree with him. He knew his son was good at doing real estate deals. In fact, Roger was great at doing real estate deals. If he felt this strongly about his investing, Roger's dad would be on board as well. With his dad's blessing, Roger just needed to know how to get the ball rolling. Fearing the process would very complicated, he was extremely relieved to learn that using retirement money to invest in real estate was actually a piece of cake.

Step One: Open an Account

The first thing Roger had to do was to open an individual 401(k) account. He interviewed a few different self-directed custodians that had been recommended to him and picked one that seemed to have good service and reasonable fees.

Step Two: Fund the Account

Once the account was open, Roger funded his individual 401(k). With a net income of $90,000, he was able to put $40,000 into the account. He simply wrote a check to the individual 401(k), and the money went straight into the retirement account. Once the funds had transferred, we finished his tax returns, and Roger was happy to see that the taxes due had immediately reduced by $13,000. This meant more cash in his pocket to invest in even more deals.

Step Three: Invest

Once the $40,000 was in the retirement account, the last step was to actually invest it. Roger found a small cottage that was for sale and immediately knew it was a hidden gem with a lot of great upside potential. He contacted the retirement custodians to let them know this was a property he was interested in, and they took care of the paperwork for him. Soon the property had been purchased, a tenant in place, and the cash flowing in.

The moral of the story is that diversification may or may not be a good thing; it really depends on the investor. For someone like Roger, who has unique advantages with regard to investing in real estate, it makes sense for him to have more of his money in real estate than in other assets he has no knowledge of or control over. Whether it's diversification or specialization, always invest in what you know best.

What Does All This Mean?

We find it outrageous that the IRS has allowed self-directed investing for more than 30 years, yet most Americans have still never heard of it. In fact, many CPAs and financial advisors may not be familiar with it, either.

Retirement contributing is one of the most powerful tools in the tax world, because it allows you to put money toward your retirement rather than paying it to the IRS. With the added benefit of tax-deferred growth, retirement strategies often provide significant short-term and long-term tax benefits.

Now that you know one of the best kept secrets to retirement investing—one that Wall Street doesn't want you to know—the door to opportunity is wide open. And remember, diversification is not always the key when investing. Always invest in what you know best.

Using Retirement Accounts to Fund Your Investments

With a self-directed IRA you can invest your retirement savings outside of Wall Street.... One of the best-kept secrets that Wall Street doesn't necessarily want you to know about.

– Kaaren Hall
Self-Directed Investing Expert

Life is unfair, and so are taxes. We all know about the benefits of saving for retirement, right? Put money into an IRA or a Roth IRA each year, and let that money grow on a tax-deferred basis until retirement. But did you know that not all retirement accounts are created equally? Although the IRA and the Roth IRA do provide some pretty good tax advantages, there are lesser-known retirement accounts that can provide significantly better tax benefits. Let's take a look at how another type of retirement account might help you supercharge your wealth building.

Tapping into Retirement Money for Real Estate Deals

Real Life: When Bob first started investing in real estate, his col-leagues on the police force all thought he was crazy. When he shared his plans to borrow against his home equity to purchase his first rehab deal, some of his closest friends tried their best to talk him out of it. It wasn't without good reason, of course. Most of his long-time friends thought that getting into real estate was risky business, especially because everyone had recently seen on the news that a real estate tycoon from New York City had just filed for bankruptcy for the third time as a result of the latest real estate downturn. However, Bob felt that he had found the perfect investment opportunity in his own backyard. Just down the street, a small house on a large lot was for sale, and it was exactly what Bob was looking for. After finding out it was zoned for a fourplex, he decided, against the advice of his colleagues, friends, and family, to move forward with purchasing this small property.

Thanks to that new property, just one year later, Bob was at the station with his colleagues celebrating his early retirement. It was not an easy decision for Bob to retire early from the police force. He was not retiring because he had struck gold and become the next real estate tycoon overnight. The truth was, Bob was quitting his job out of desperation so he could focus his attention on the property.

The previous year had been a very difficult one for Bob. He was working full-time and spent his time off managing his fourplex. Real estate was much harder than Bob had ever imagined. Rehabbing the property, construction additions, and managing contractors were no easy feats. From time to time, he would enlist his teenage sons to assist with hammering a few nails or carrying cement. He was burnt out trying to juggle both jobs and ready for a change in his day job. He wanted to focus all his efforts on his new real estate venture. Bob packed up his desk at the office so he could finish the renovations on his property and see where his new investment took him.

In the end, it was worth all the aching muscles and sleepless nights. Once the improvements were done, Bob's property increased in value by close to $170,000. Rather than selling it and paying the taxes, Bob followed our recommendation to keep it as a rental for a few years. His long-term goal was to eventually trade up to an apartment building in Dayton, Ohio. We explained that he might be able to permanently defer the taxes on any capital gains by using a 1031 exchange to upgrade his real estate down the road, whenever he was ready for a switch. Bob liked this idea and welcomed the tax savings. In addition, the cash flow was looking good for the fourplex, already coming in at close to $4,000 per month. After all his hard work, Bob had actually replaced the income he had lost by leaving his day job at the station.

After discovering his property's significant increase in value, Bob took out a loan to borrow against the equity in that property and used that money to do some smaller fix-and-flip deals on the side. All in all, things were looking pretty good for Bob. The real estate market was still low in his market area, so he knew that this was the time to buy. The only hurdle was that his cash was limited, and with his W-2 income gone, Bob found that his ability to get a loan was limited as well.

At a local Real Estate Investors Association meeting, Dan approached Bob and introduced himself. Dan was a seasoned investor with a real wealth of information, and the two stayed in touch. Bob enjoyed picking Dan's brain about ideas ranging from how to deal with contractors to tricks for getting the best price on materials. But the golden nugget Bob learned from Dan the night they first met was how to use retirement money for real estate investments.

According to Dan, this was called self-directed investing. Now that Bob had left the police force, he was able to move his money from his old 401(k) into a self-directed IRA account. Once the money was in the new account, Bob would be able to use it to invest in rental real estate and increase his returns.

This was music to his ears. There was over $140,000 in his 401(k) that was sitting in the stock market, which made Bob uneasy. The idea of using retirement money for real estate deals via self-directed investing was definitely something Bob wanted to learn more about. He knew we had spoken with him about the concept a few months earlier but could not exactly recall the pros and cons we had discussed.

This was the first year Bob worked full-time in real estate, so it was hard for him to predict just how much income he would make in terms of flip profits. Going forward, Bob's income would come mainly from two sources: rental income from the fourplex and fix-and-flip income from deals he would do on the side. What was clear in Bob's mind was that he definitely wanted to take advantage of using his 401(k) money for real estate. Now he just needed to know where to open the account.

Knowing Your Options

There was so much more Bob could do beyond simply moving money from his 401(k) into a self-directed IRA and then buying rental property. Who would have guessed he had options to consider and even more strategies he could use?

Real estate investors all love the concept of leverage. Knowing that Bob would enjoy taking advantage of new types of leverage, we asked if he would be interested in using the $140,000 in his retirement account to purchase $280,000 worth of real estate. Bob's answer? "Yes, please!"

He had had no idea that such a thing was possible. Bob learned that a handful of banks and lending institutions would actually lend money to self-directed retirement accounts. So rather than using the $140,000 to pay all cash for one rental property, he might be able to use the $140,000 as down payment on two rental properties and get bank financing for the remaining $140,000. This sounded almost too good to be true, and in fact, there are potentially big taxes associated when you leverage your retirement money.

A tax called the Unrelated Debt-Financed Income (UDFI) tax can be assessed when leveraging strategies are used within a retirement account. This little-known tax sometimes catches investors off guard and can be 39.6% in some cases.

You may be thinking, "How can there be taxes within a retirement account? Isn't that unconstitutional?" Well, unfortunately, it's not. The IRS does allow an IRA to use leverage to invest in an asset. However, the IRS assesses 39.6% tax on any taxable income generated as a result of the debt. Let's look at an example.

If you purchased a rental property inside your retirement of $200,000 with $80,000 cash and $120,000 bank financing, this means the investment is 60% leveraged. If the net taxable income from this property after taking depreciation and all other write-offs ends up being $12,000 this year, roughly $7,200 of the current-year profit may be subject to the UDFI tax, currently up to as much as a 39.6% tax rate. (The UDFI tax is imposed on a sliding scale, with rates ranging from 15% to 39.6%; however, for simplicity, we will use 39.6% in our example, which follows.)

UDFI Calculation

$12,000 Current-Year Taxable Income

60% Leverage

$7,200
($1,000) Exemption
$6,200 UDFI Taxable Income
39.6% Tax Rate
$2,455 Taxes Due

For Bob, however, the bad news ends here. We had another trick up our sleeve that would help him use leverage and yet escape this tax altogether using a different type of self-directed retirement account known as the Solo 401(k).

The Solo 401(k), sometimes known as a Solo(k), is a more flexible and more powerful type of self-directed account. Using a Solo(k), Bob would be able to purchase a rental property using leverage without having to worry about UDFI taxes of 39.6%, regardless of how much debt he had on the property. For example, if he wanted to roll his current retirement account of $140,000 into a Solo(k) and use that as his 20% down payment to buy a multifamily apartment worth $700,000, there would be zero UDFI taxes for Bob to worry about. All the cash flow from Bob's apartment investment would go back into his Solo(k) account free of current UDFI taxes. If he were to sell that apartment, he still wouldn't have to worry about any taxes on gains as long as the money stayed in the retirement account.

Another perk of the Solo(k), one that is not available with an IRA, is the ability to borrow money from it. Bob had indicated that he needed some extra money to do another fix-and-flip deal. Our strategy for Bob was that if he needed extra money from his retirement account on a short-term basis to fund his deals, he could take out a loan from his Solo(k) and use that money. As long as Bob committed to repaying his Solo(k) with interest on a fully amortized schedule and within a five-year period, this strategy would allow Bob to access his retirement money on a tax-free and penalty-free basis.

This was music to his ears. After all, Bob loved the idea of borrowing from his retirement account and paying interest to himself rather than to a bank or private lender.

Bob was so relieved that he had come in to meet with us before simply moving his money over to a self-directed IRA as Dan had suggested. He could already see the benefits of the Solo(k) over an IRA. Just when he thought he knew everything there was to know about the Solo(k), we gave him one more piece of great tax-saving advice.

In addition to Bob's being able to leverage the Solo(k) and borrow from it tax-free and penalty-free, the Solo(k) also offered him a higher contribution limit than other IRA accounts.

For example, if Bob earned $50,000 in flip profits that year, rather than contributing the usual $5,500 into his IRA and taking a $5,500 tax deduction, he could contribute $27,500 into a Solo(k) and take a $27,500 tax write-off. Based on his tax rate of 30%, this would save him close to $8,250 in income taxes just the first year. The other benefit was that Bob would have an extra $27,500 in his retirement account that he could use to invest in real estate.

To make sure he understood some of the major differences between an IRA and a Solo(k), Bob asked us to create a comparison chart illustrating both options side by side.

	Self-Directed IRA	Self-Directed Solo(k)
Can Invest in Leveraged Real Estate	Yes	Yes
Avoidance of UDFI Taxes	No	Yes
Tax-Free Borrowing?	No	Yes
Penalty-Free Borrowing?	No	Yes
Maximum Contribution Limit (under 50 yrs. old)	$5,500	$53,000

Bob loved this new super retirement account. It sounded like a no-brainer to him; he should be able to put as much money into his retirement account as possible to both lower his taxes and have more money growing for him on a tax-deferred basis. To him, it was just like moving money from his left pocket to his right pocket and getting a tax deduction for doing it. Now the only question Bob had was how hard it would be to set up this retirement account.

To his surprise, the account setup was not much harder than it would have been for an IRA. In fact, the account setup process was exactly the same. The custodian Bob initially intended to use to open his self-directed IRA was also able to set up self-directed 401(k) accounts. Bob simply filled out some paperwork and authorized the transfer of money from his old employer account into his new self-directed Solo(k) account. Within a few days, the money was in Bob's new account, and he was ready to put that money to work!

What Does All This Mean?

As you may know by now, the U.S. tax code is a complex set of laws and regulations that stump even the smartest people in our country. However, if you know how to apply the code to your particular situation, you can take advantage of a large number of loopholes to legally reduce your tax burden. Sometimes even a small change can result in significant tax savings.

By combining retirement investing and the concept of leverage, an investor may be able to accelerate their path to retirement. Numerous types of retirement accounts, self-directed strategies, and retirement rollover options can be used to put your money into real estate deals. Before you fund your retirement account this year, speak with your tax advisor on what "type" of account would be best for your situation.

One Big and Costly Mistake

A Jack of all trades is a master of none.

— Unknown

There is no such thing as a "tax guru." In other words, no one single person in the United States can claim to know everything about the U.S. tax code. That would be impossible. Have you ever met a health care guru? Someone who can clean your teeth, deliver your baby, and do heart and brain surgery on you at the same time? Of course not! The heart surgeon went to school for years and years and worked thousands of hours to fine-tune their skills in heart surgery. He is probably not the best person to choose when you need your teeth cleaned or a baby delivered.

Meet Jack (Of All Trades)

One of the biggest issues we see in our accounting profession is that, unfortunately for many taxpayers, a lot of advisors fall into the jack-of-all-trades category. You see, setting up an accounting business is actually pretty easy. In fact, tax preparers don't even need a college degree; a large percentage of the people who prepare tax returns at the franchise-type locations have neither a degree nor any advanced tax or accounting knowledge.

You may wonder, "What about someone who has gone through the most extensive training and obtained their CPA license and met all the education and work experience requirements? Does that make them an expert in all tax matters?" Of course not! The tax code and its complexities are simply too much for one individual to know completely.

However, we often see individuals, whether licensed or not, open an accounting and tax office and just start advertising for clients. After all, there's a very low barrier of entry for this business. Your biggest expense in opening an accounting and tax business is probably rent—which you can avoid if you work from home. You probably also need a laptop and some office supplies such as paper and paper clips, right? Oh, we forgot a calculator! Yes, you do need a calculator.

Assuming the person has great marketing skills, potential clients will come knocking as soon as the business is open. It is generally hard to turn away clients, and this goes for accounting and tax businesses as well. National statistics show that the average one-person tax company has approximately 700 clients, if not more. Those clients can represent many different types of tax profiles, such as W-2 employees, consultants, owners of restaurants or manufacturing companies, and of course, real estate investors.

This means that to provide the best service, the tax advisor should keep up-to-date on all the changes for these areas within the tax code. Not only do they need to know how to take advantage of the latest manufacturing tax credits, but they also need to know about tax credits for physicians who work in remote, rural locations, as well as the latest depreciation rules for improvements made to a rental property. Each of these tax benefits is buried within its own set of complex rules, exceptions, and loopholes. On top of that, the average preparer works about 18 hours a day during tax season, so it is no wonder that a lot of tax deductions and loopholes are missed.

Let's be honest, have you ever met a CPA or tax person who told you they couldn't help you because they didn't understand real estate taxes? If you did, that would be an exception and extremely rare. In fact, you should count your lucky stars if someone has told you they couldn't help you with your taxes because they didn't understand or specialize in real estate. This honest and trustworthy person may have saved you thousands of dollars in taxes by telling you the truth.

In the real word, most tax advisors will likely tell you that they understand real estate. Not only can they help you with your real estate taxes, but they can also help with your brother's restaurant business, if your brother is looking for a CPA, too.

It would be nice to have a jack-of-all trades tax advisor, right? At the very least, that person could be a kind of one-stop shop where you and your brother could both go to get your taxes done at the same time. How specialized does your CPA really need to be? After all, taxes are taxes, right?

Something Doesn't Add Up

Real Life: *Our client Darren is a Bostonian who raised seven sons by working in the welding business for more than 25 years. After hearing us speak on an educational podcast, he sent us an email to ask if we could help him. Now let me warn you, this story is not a happy one—definitely not one of those feel-good, chicken-soup-for-the-soul types of stories we've been telling you so far. If you are brave enough to read a real story about how a real estate investor could lose a ton of money because of a small mistake, keep reading.*

We received the following email from Darren:

My name is Darren, and I retired early from welding a year ago to sit in the sun, or so I thought. My wife and I moved away from the harsh New England winters to work on our tan in sunny Florida.

While managing my investments over the past year, it has become crystal clear to me that I need to invest in real estate to build wealth, so as of early December, I have begun taking steps to abandon the stock market. I have purchased a few properties and plan on buying more before the year is over. I really need someone to help me on this journey.

Let me know if this is something you can help me with. I'm not sure if it is too late, but we paid Uncle Sam $30,000 in taxes this year and still owe him $66,000. I did not have a business last year, and we are both retired, so I didn't have any money to use to start my real estate investing aside from my work 401(k) money.

I look forward to hearing from you.

As soon as we read this email, we knew we needed to speak with Darren immediately. It didn't make sense that someone with his profile—who had recently retired, did not own a business, and had no other income—would owe more than $96,000 in taxes. It just didn't add up. Owing this much in taxes would mean that Darren, this self-proclaimed retired (and tanned) gentleman, had somehow made more than $300,000 in income that he had to pay taxes on.

Did he get some sort of large severance check like big corporate executives do? That's not something you commonly see in the welding industry. Also, Darren didn't mention anything about severance pay. Could he have received a large vacation payout when he left his employer? This was also not likely, unless his company had paid him for years and years of accrued vacation. None of the numbers really made sense to us. The only other thing he mentioned in his email was his 401(k), which was the only source of cash he could use for real estate investing. We had some theories about why his tax bill was so high, and unfortunately, when we spoke with Darren, he confirmed exactly what we had feared.

About a month into his retirement, Darren felt like he was losing control of his finances. Watching the stock market rise and fall every day made him uneasy, so he decided to take matters into his own hands when he heard about a real estate investment conference just a few miles from his house. At the conference, Darren met all sorts of real estate investors from across the United States. It was an eye-opening experience, and he quickly learned that if he wanted to have more control over his money and build a legacy to pass on to his kids and grandkids, he should consider adding some real estate to his investment portfolio. According to the expert who taught a breakout class during the conference, one of the emerging markets that would likely show a large appreciation in the next five years was none other than sunny Florida. "Not a bad idea," Darren thought. What better way to start than to invest in his own backyard? A few of the teachers taught some creative financing techniques, which really piqued Darren's interest, given that he didn't have a pile of cash with which to jump-start his investing at that time. This was why he was so excited to learn at the conference that using retirement money for real estate investments could be a good idea.

Traditionally, people put the retirement money in their 401(k)s and IRAs into the stock market or mutual funds. However, the experts at the real estate conference apparently thought that real estate was a great place to invest retirement money as well.

Early the next morning, Darren contacted his retirement custodian and told them he wanted to use his money to purchase some rental properties. To his surprise, the investment custodian told him he was not allowed to do this. Shocked and disappointed by this response, Darren didn't understand why he couldn't. He was pretty sure one of the instructors at the conference had told him he could use retirement money to buy rental properties and that there was some benefit to doing so, though Darren couldn't exactly remember what.

To get to the bottom of the issue, Darren contacted his CPA in Boston, who was an old family friend who had helped Darren and his parents file taxes for over a decade. In fact, Darren seemed to remember that his CPA also owned a few rental properties. He felt that he was the best person to ask.

Unfortunately, the CPA did not have good news for Darren. He agreed with the investment firm's conclusion that there was no way for Darren to use his 401(k) money to purchase rental real estate. It simply was impossible with his existing account. The CPA suggested a work-around in which Darren would take his retirement money out of the 401(k) and simply pay the taxes on it. Then, Darren could invest in whatever he wanted to.

Although this was not the best news, Darren took his CPA and investment advisor's advice and called the retirement custodian to liquidate his account. Darren believed this was the only way he could get a large sum of cash to jump-start his real estate venture, so at the time, it seemed like a great move. Over the next several months, he did fairly well for himself and bought a few single-family homes, which he fixed up and rented out.

The Shocking Reality

Not until tax time did Darren realize he had a problem. When his tax returns were done for that year, his CPA told him he owed close to $96,000 in taxes. According to the CPA, Darren's liquidation of $200,000 of 401(k) money earlier that year had resulted in federal income taxes. In addition, because Darren was under the age of fifty-five when he received the retirement distributions, he was also subject to a 10% penalty fee on the withdrawn money.

This was terrible news for Darren, and he was not prepared for this bill. He had already used every penny of that 401(k) money for his new rental properties. Even though the cash flow he had received from these new rentals over the past few months had been good, it was nowhere near what he needed to send to the IRS.

This was the precise reason he had contacted us. He was desperately hoping that we could somehow help him avoid or reduce this tax bill.

Unfortunately for Darren, it was too late for us to help him unring that bell. By the time he contacted us, all the paperwork had been executed, and the money was firmly invested into real estate deals. The only thing he could do at that time was try to maximize all the expenses he had incurred on his rental properties and accelerate the depreciation on the improvements he had made.

Had Darren's CPA been better informed and more familiar with real estate and investment strategies, he would have advised Darren to simply move his 401(k) money into an IRA with a self-directed custodian and then use the new account for his real estate investments. When the investment firm told Darren he could not invest 401(k) money into rental real estate, that was misleading. The truth was that their specific investment firm did not have a way for Darren to do this. The types of assets—generally stocks, bonds, and mutual funds—the firm provided limited Darren's investment choices. He did not realize that if he had simply moved his account to a new firm, he might have a much wider variety of investment choices.

A Small Mistake that Cost Big-Time

The IRS has no restriction that requires you to put your 401(k) money into the stock market. As we have explained, it is perfectly legal for someone to use retirement money for real estate deals. You simply need to transfer your money to the right custodians who can help you do so. These special custodians are referred to as "self-directed" retirement custodians. "Self-directed" simply means that you can choose where you invest your retirement money. In a truly self-directed IRA, the custodian does not give you a list of investment choices. Instead, you get to choose whatever you want to invest in, whether that be rental properties, start-up businesses, notes, liens, etc.

Now the IRS does specify a few things you cannot invest your retirement money in, such as life insurance contracts and collectible items. But for the most part, self-directed investing means you have 100% control over where your retirement money is invested. Therefore, you could use your retirement money to buy that new property on the market on Main Street or to invest in your cousin's new start-up Internet business.

Often we have clients who will call their investment firm and ask to move their money into self-directed account, only to be told they already have a self-directed IRA. Some financial planners will tell clients that in their

IRA, the client can choose whatever they want to invest in, so it is already self-directed. How do you know if you are being misled? Here is a quick tip:

If the firm offers you a list of investment choices, you do not have a self-directed account.

Self-directed retirement means you choose what you want to invest in; you do not select an option from a predetermined list of choices.

Again, had Darren simply moved his money from the 401(k) into a self-directed IRA, he would have been able to avoid his tax issue altogether. Not only could he have rolled his 401(k) money into a traditional IRA in a tax-free manner to later purchase his new rental properties, but also, any rental income he would earn over the next several years could grow tax deferred in his retirement account. Thus, the mistake Darren made by simply liquidating his 401(k) cost him more than $96,000 in taxes and penalties. He also missed out on a great opportunity for tax-deferred growth.

Had Darren's CPA been a tax expert in the self-directed arena, he would have advised Darren to do the following:

Step 1: Find a good self-directed custodian and set up a self-directed IRA account.

Step 2: Fill out the paperwork for the self-directed custodian to request that 401(k) funds be directly transferred into the new self-directed IRA.

Step 3: Use the funds in the self-directed IRA to purchase rental real estate and pay for any necessary property improvements.

Step 4: Earn rental income in the self-directed IRA to allow for tax-deferred growth.

Darren's CPA may have been familiar with real estate–related taxes, but he was not an expert in self-directed IRA–related strategies. Because of this lack of knowledge, his incorrect advice cost Darren a great deal of money that could have otherwise been saved.

Just as you would not want your dentist to diagnose your chest pain, you would not want to work with a tax advisor who does not specialize in the areas where you need assistance the most. If you ever receive advice that doesn't make sense to you, it doesn't hurt to get a second or third opinion, just to make sure your bases are covered. Learning something too late can often be a costly, but avoidable, mistake.

How to Know if You Are Working with the Right Tax Advisor

Here are a few tips to help you easily and quickly determine whether you are working with the right tax advisor for your particular situation:

1. Avoid the glazed look: If your CPA gets a glazed look on their face when you start talking about real estate or you find yourself having to explain your real estate transactions year after year, you may be working with the wrong person. Yes, we all do creative real estate transactions from time to time, but your CPA should know the basic transactions within your industry.

2. Who's the CPA: It is okay for you to tell your CPA from time to time about a new tax loophole you've heard about. Maybe you just attended a seminar and learned of a new, cutting-edge idea that your tax advisors weren't yet aware of. But if you are bringing ideas to your CPA more often than they brings ideas to you (i.e., you feel like you are the CPA), you may not be working with the right person.

3. Giving you leverage: Your tax advisor should be someone who can help you with more than just taxes. They should also be able to share what they see in the market, what other investors have been doing that has been successful, and how other people have been able to raise money. You should be able to leverage your CPA's knowledge and experience to supercharge your investing plans.

What Does All This Mean?

Taxes and finances are topics that are very private and personal to each of us. In addition to finding someone who specializes in working with people like you, make sure you find someone you trust and feel comfortable talking with. You should be well acquainted with your advisor and be able to have open and honest communication with them to obtain the most value for your relationship and financial well-being. Know the key points to look out for to ensure you are working with the right person. When in doubt, get a second or third opinion. Remember, you cannot unring a bell.

IRS PITFALLS

Depreciation: A Powerful Tax Tool for Real Estate Investors

Intaxication: euphoria at getting a refund from the IRS, which lasts until you realize it was your money to start with.

—Greg Oetjen

Depreciation is a common strategy available to just about every business owner and real estate investor. It can be a powerful tool when it comes to reducing tax liabilities year after year.

It may be shocking to hear that a deduction that helps investors save thousands of dollars in tax is sometimes overlooked. Unfortunately, the reality is that this does happen more often than you might think.

> **Real Life:** *Several years before Emma retired from her long-time job, she made the decision to invest in rental properties to generate some passive income to supplement her during retirement. By the time Emma left her job, she had invested in ten single family and multi-family homes. The properties did not do very well at first, and most of her profits went back into repairs and improvements. A few years into her investing career, Emma's properties started making money, and Emma was glad to finally see the benefits of being a real estate investor. In her first year of generating good cash flow, Emma was informed by her tax preparer about some bad news: She owed over*

119

$11,000 in taxes to the IRS!

Without much cash on hand, Emma called up her lender and asked to refinance one of her rental properties so that she could take cash out to pay the taxes due. After speaking with Emma, one of the first things that the lender wanted to do was to take a look at her tax return to verify income. Luckily, Emma's lender was someone who worked quite a bit with real estate investors. The lender had reviewed many tax returns before and immediately knew that something was off. The lender quickly contacted us and brought us in for a second opinion on what he had seen.

After spending just a few minutes with Emma and her lender, we confirmed that Emma had been missing out on her depreciation for all of her rental properties.

As you can imagine, Emma was in extreme shock. How was it possible that her CPA did not take depreciation? Wasn't it his job to calculate that for her? After all, he was the tax expert that she entrusted to do her taxes all these years, right? Emma could not believe what we were telling her. Staring at the tax return line labeled as "depreciation," Emma noticed those fields were indeed blank for each and every single one of her rental properties.

What is Depreciation?

The IRS defines depreciation as "an income tax deduction that allows a taxpayer to recover the cost or other basis of certain property."

Yuck. That doesn't make a whole lot of sense, does it?

Let's use an analogy. Depreciation can be more easily explained in an example with cars. You may have heard that as soon as you drive a new car off the dealer's lot, it loses some of its value. It is true that after you purchase a car, the value begins to decline or depreciate over time, and it is generally worth less each year. While this doesn't seem like a particularly good thing, it actually can be a benefit when it comes to taxes. The IRS allows taxpayers to write off this decrease in value of the car as a business expense each year via tax depreciation.

The same type of tax benefit applies to those who invest in rentals and certain other types of real estate deals. The depreciation benefit for real estate investors is that the IRS allows taxpayers to depreciate the purchase price of the building each year as a tax deduction. While it is easy to see the value of a car depreciate over time, rental real estate is a different story. Historically speaking, real estate values can increase over time, correct? So how is depreciation for rental properties impacted in years when the property increases in value? The answer is that it is not impacted at all. The IRS allows investors to take depreciation deductions for rental properties even in years when the properties appreciate in value!

Here are some important things to note about depreciation of rental real estate:

- Depreciation is taken each year that the property is actively in service as a rental.

- The same depreciation is taken whether the property value increases or decreases during the year.

- Depreciation is generally taken based on the purchase price of the property regardless of its current fair market value.

- Depreciation is calculated based on your total purchase price of the investment property, regardless of what your down payment is.

As you can see from the bullet points above, depreciation can be a powerful tax write-off. It is not impacted by or associated with how the real estate market is doing as a whole. For rental real estate investors, there are two main criteria that must be met in order to take tax depreciation.

First, you must own the property. If you are not the property owner and are simply renting from a landlord just to sublease a property out to someone else, you may not take depreciation on that property.

Second, the property must be an income-producing property. The most common example of this would be a piece of real estate that is generating rental income. Accordingly, there is generally no depreciation on your primary home or your second/vacation home if no income is generated from the property.

For real estate investors, the building is not the only item that is depreciable. Many other assets that have a useful life of over one year can potentially be eligible for tax depreciation. Each type of asset has a depreciable "life" that the IRS designates. The "life" of an asset dictates how many years it will take for the asset to be fully depreciated. Here is a chart of some common useful lives for residential rental real estate:

Light Fixtures	5 Years	Carpet & Flooring	5 Years
Furniture	5 Years	Appliances	5 Years
Cabinets	5 Years	Land Improvements	15 Years
Remodels	27.5 Years	Countertops	27.5 Years
Windows	27.5 Years	Doors	27.5 Years
Improvements	27.5 Years	HVAC	27.5 Years
Residential Building	27.5 Years	Water Heaters	27.5 Years
Commercial Building	39 Years	Land (not depreciable)	0 Years

For example, if you install new carpet for $1,000 for your rental property, then you may be able to take a portion of the depreciation each year as a tax deduction. In five years, you would have taken a total accumulated depreciation of $1,000 based on the IRS depreciation table. Once the accumulated depreciation is equal to the basis or purchase price, then the adjusted basis of the carpet would be zero.

Calculating Depreciation

One of the pitfalls to watch out for when calculating depreciation for your rental property is to make sure that you break out your purchase price between land and building. Why is it important to split out land versus building? The reason is because although a building is depreciable under the tax code, land is not.

Land does not depreciate because the IRS deems that it does not go down in value over time. It does not experience normal wear and tear like appliances, furniture, or buildings do. Accordingly, since the building portion is depreciable and land is not, they cannot be depreciated as one asset and must be split up on your tax returns.

Now, if you have looked on a closing settlement HUD, you will notice that generally the purchase price is shown as one lump sum, and there is no separately stated amount for land versus building. Here are a few simple ways for you to determine the land versus building allocation for your rental property.

One way to do this is to find the land and building allocation information on your appraisal report. If an appraiser breaks out the land versus building percentage on an official appraisal report, that allocation may be used by you to determine the portion of the purchase price of your property that is associated with the depreciable building.

Another way to determine the land versus building breakout can be to contact the tax assessor's office for the county where the property is located. Many counties will have this information on their website readily available. Other times, you may even be able to find the land versus building value on your property tax bill. Once you know how to split up the land and building, you can depreciate the building on your tax return.

For example, let's say that you purchased a rental property for $500,000, and the county tax assessor determined that 40% is attributed to land and 60% is attributed to buildings and improvements. The calculation of land versus building would be as follows:

$500,000 Purchase Price x 40% = $200,000 Land Value

$500,000 Purchase Price x 60% = $300,000 Building Value

In this scenario, you would have $200,000 of land that is not depreciable and $300,000 of building that has a life of 27.5 years. This results in a depreciation expense of $10,909 per year. If you are someone in the 28% tax bracket, this depreciation alone can save you up to $3,054 in taxes each year.

One mistake that investors and some tax preparers make is that they forget to include the land value on the returns. Some feel that since land is not depreciable, why put that on the tax return or depreciation schedule?

Just because land isn't depreciable doesn't mean it's not important. In the example above, if you only include the $300,000 of building on your tax returns, then when you sell your property a few years later, your taxable gain on the tax return may show $200,000 more gain than what is appropriate. If the land never was shown on the tax return as part of your original cost, how will you show it as part of your purchase price and cost basis when you sell it? Showing land on the tax return depreciation schedule, even though it does not depreciate every year, helps you to minimize the risk of over-reporting your gain. That is why it is essential to track both the land and the building cost basis to make sure that you do not end up paying more tax than what is necessary.

As you can see, depreciation can be a very powerful tax tool when it comes to real estate investing. How exactly does depreciation work when you sell a property down the road? Let's say that you bought a rental property for $100,000, and over the years, you took $20,000 of depreciation. When you sell your property for $130,000, instead of having a gain of $30,000, it can actually be a tax gain of $50,000. Although your original cost basis was $100,000, your adjusted basis is decreased by the depreciation that you have already taken over the years. Let's illustrate below:

Purchase Price	$100,000
Accumulated Depreciation	($20,000)
Adjusted Basis	$80,000
Sale Price	$130,000
Adjusted Basis	($80,000)
Gain on Sale	$50,000

The reason that depreciation that has been taken on prior year tax returns increases your tax gain when the property is sold is because depreciation represents a portion of your purchase price that has already reduced your taxes. Many investors are not aware of this effect on gains and are often quite surprised when they sell their properties and end up with an unexpected gain on their tax return. Using the same example as above, if the investor sold the property for the same price that they bought it for, there could still be a gain because of the depreciation expense taken previously.

Purchase Price	$100,000
Accumulated Depreciation	($20,000)
Adjusted Basis	$80,000
Sale Price (same as purchase price)	$100,000
Adjusted Basis	($80,000)
Gain on Sale	$20,000

Taxes can be complicated, and you never want to end up with an unexpected IRS bill at tax time. This is an excellent example of why it is important to consult with your tax advisor prior to selling a property.

We do sometimes come across investors who say they don't want to take depreciation. Maybe they have enough other expenses to offset the rental income each year, or maybe calculating depreciation is just too complicated. More often than not, we come across investors who are advised by their CPA to not take depreciation and instead "save it up" for future years. This type of advice can be extremely detrimental to real estate investors for one main reason:

Depreciation is not a choice.

A depreciation deduction is something that is required under the tax law. As indicated above, the tax code provides very specific methods and timeframes for how each asset must be depreciated. This means that the choice to take a depreciation deduction or not is not at the discretion of the taxpayer. For example, if we bought a rental property, we cannot simply choose to skip deducting depreciation for the first five years and then depreciate all of it in year six. The annual depreciation amount must be calculated and taken according to the rules set forth by the IRS.

In fact, what many investors may not know is that when you sell an investment property, the IRS will calculate your tax gain as if you took the necessary depreciation every single year. In our example above, if you were required to take $20,000 of depreciation over the years but simply chose not to, there could still potentially be a $20,000 tax gain when it comes time to sell that investment property. For this reason, it makes absolutely no sense not to take depreciation each year.

If you are someone who has enough expenses to offset your rental income and do not need depreciation, take it anyway. In that scenario, the depreciation may create a net loss for your rentals, and that loss may be carried into future years to offset future rental income.

Accelerated Depreciation

Although the IRS has a set of depreciation lives and methods for each particular asset, there is an advanced depreciation strategy that may be available to many investors. One way to potentially reduce a large portion of an investor's taxable income is by using accelerated depreciation. This is done via a process commonly known as a cost segregation study.

A cost segregation study allows you to break down the building portion of your rental property into smaller assets with shorter lives. How does this work? Well, the building portion of your rental property includes everything that you are purchasing except for the land. This includes kitchen counters, cabinets, toilets, light fixtures, and on and on. If the building portion of your rental is $300,000 and a cost segregation is not performed, then you are generally depreciating the $300,000 over 27.5 years.

With a cost segregation study, you can instead break out all of these other building components and depreciate each component over their shorter useful life. For example, it may look something like this:

$200,000	25 year assets—Building, Improvements, HVAC
$70,000	5 year assets—Fixtures, Furniture, Flooring
$30,000	15 year assets—Landscaping, Fencing, Sidewalks
$300,000	Total "Building"

Accelerated depreciation is a powerful tool that can significantly reduce an investor's tax liability. You will get the same amount of total depreciation expense over the entire life of the building, but now with a cost segregation study, you could get to deduct some of your purchase price a lot sooner! However, it may not be a great strategy for everyone. One potential downside is that cost segregation studies can be costly and time consuming. If you have a time constraint, such as an IRS bill or an upcoming filing deadline, then you may not have enough time to complete one.

Another item to consider is the cost versus benefit of having a cost segregation done. With a cost segregation, the tax benefit of a single family home purchased for $150,000 can be significantly different from fourplex purchased for $400,000. Before spending money to get a cost segregation done for your rentals, make sure you work with your tax advisor to determine how much in taxes it will save you. If you are going to spend more on the cost segregation study than you are going to receive in tax savings, it may not be a great idea.

How Do I Know if I Am Missing Out on Depreciation?

For many years, Emma missed out on the depreciation benefits of her rental properties. What was worse was that she had no idea that she was getting bad advice from her CPA. Fortunately for Emma, she found a savvy mortgage lender who noticed an issue and promptly pointed her in the right direction. We helped her to file an amended tax return by calculating what her basis in the properties should have been and claimed depreciation for that year on her taxes. Luckily for Emma, her taxable income was reduced to zero, and her tax liability was reduced to zero. Emma was happy because she didn't owe money to the IRS anymore.

How can you ensure you don't fall into the same predicament as Emma? How can you tell if you have been taking depreciation on your tax returns? Well, it's simple. On each tax return where the rental income and expenses are reported each year, there is a specific line with "depreciation" as the description. If you are wondering whether you have claimed depreciation on your rentals, one of the easiest things to do is to pull out your most recent tax return. Scan the page where your rental activities are shown, and go down to the "depreciation" line. If there is no amount indicated there, that could be a sign that you are missing out on this wonderful deduction. If you don't see an expense listed on the depreciation line of your tax return, it may be a good idea to get a second opinion from another tax advisor.

What Does All This Mean?

Although depreciation is just one of the many tax savings tools, it is one that can provide a significant tax impact for investors. Depreciation taken correctly can be the difference between a large tax liability and a large tax refund. Depreciation can often be thousands of dollars per property each year, so we aren't talking about pocket change. As you can see from Emma's ordeal, it can have a dramatic effect on your tax bill.

Although hard for most taxpayers to believe, the tax code actually provides a lot of deductions that benefit taxpayers. The trick is just making sure that you take full advantage of them. Work with tax advisors who specialize in the real estate industry, and lean on them for their expertise and guidance.

How to Gift Properties to Your Family and Not the IRS

The best kind of money to leave to your heirs is the tax-free kind. That and the legacy of knowledge and power to create wealth on their own accord.

—Bruce Norris,
Real Estate Investor

For most of us, the goal of working hard and investing seriously is not necessarily to become rich. It is not to drive the nicest car on the block or have the biggest house in the neighborhood. Instead, the "purpose" of our wealth building can be summed up in one word: legacy. It is the legacy we want to leave our kids and grandkids that drives a lot of us to be passionate about our real estate efforts—our desire for them to have a better life, a better education, and better opportunities.

Unfortunately, we often see investors who focus so much on creating wealth that they neglect to research what the most tax efficient ways are of passing that wealth on to future generations. Most of the time, we do not even realize we missed out on tax savings until it is too late. The good news is that it may not be too late for you. You are reading this book, so you are still alive! And that means you still have time to plan so that you leave your wealth to your beneficiaries, not to Uncle Sam.

Real Life: *It had been so hard for Jane to watch her dad's health deteriorate over the past few years. At eighty-seven years old, her dad was getting increasingly weaker physically by the day. Although he seemed to still be doing well mentally, Jane started having concerns about some of the decisions he had been making.*

About eight years earlier, Jane's dad had had his first stroke. He was no longer able to take care of himself and live independently, so Jane hired an in-home caregiver, Patti, who moved into her dad's home.

Though Patti needed some time to adjust to her new job, she adapted well and quickly learned how to care for Jane's dad. Patti figured out how to make him laugh, how to convince him to take his medicines, and most importantly, how to handle him when his temper flared. Jane was glad they got along so well, because her dad was definitely not the easiest person to deal with at times. The arrangement seemed to be going well, and Jane never had any worries, knowing her dad was in good hands. That was until a year ago, when her dad announced that he was in love with Patti, and the two were planning on getting married.

This did not sit well with Jane. Not only was Patti almost forty-five years younger than her dad, but Jane had also never seen any kind of love connection between the two. As far as she could tell, their relationship was strictly professional. Jane was not sure what Patti's true intentions were toward her father. He owned quite a few assets, including a commercial building and some smaller real estate along the coast. But even if money was not the reason behind it, Jane felt that that sort of relationship between them was unprofessional.

After the wedding announcement, things started to get worse. Jane could not get over the unease she felt about the union and tried to speak with Patti in private about her concerns. As soon as the conversation was over, Patti ran to Jane's dad to complain to him about his daughter. After that, Jane and Patti didn't speak to each other, and Jane's relationship with her dad became a bit rocky.

From that point on, Jane felt awkward around the two of them. She visited multiple times a week, but the awkwardness had changed things, and she almost felt as though she wasn't welcome in her dad's home anymore. Patti made herself scarce whenever Jane came over, and her dad remained focused on trying to get the two to reconcile. It was obvious from the way her dad acted that Patti complained about Jane quite often. Although Jane didn't know whose side her dad was on, considering his peacemaking efforts, one thing she knew for sure was that Patti considered her an enemy.

This is why Jane was so surprised when her dad called her to his bedside one day and told her he planned on giving her his commercial property. Her dad had purchased this property back in the late 1980s for just over $56,000. He didn't fully explain why he wanted to gift the property to Jane, saying only that he wanted her to have it.

Jane was filled with mixed emotions. On one hand, she was happy that her dad seemed as sharp as ever and was making this gift to ensure that he had set something aside for Jane. On the other hand, Jane saw how fragile her dad had become, and conversations like the one about the property reinforced that he would not be with her forever. Her dad indicated that he had already contacted his attorney and would be transferring the property into Jane's name as early as the following week.

Jane had never been savvy about money or investments. This would be the first time she owned an investment property, and she wanted to make sure she did everything correctly. She had heard about people forming LLCs or corporations to hold real estate, so she wanted to see about doing the same.

Sitting across from us in the conference room, Jane started telling her story from the beginning, sharing not only about the gift she was receiving, but also about the dynamics between her, her dad, and his caregiver Patti. At the end of the story, Jane reiterated that receiving this gift from her dad was something very special and she wanted to make sure everything was handled properly.

When Jane finished speaking, she immediately knew something was wrong by the concerned looks on our faces.

"You said your dad bought this property for $56,000. What is it worth today?" we asked.

"I am not positive what it would sell for today," Jane responded. "But I do know we had an appraisal done a year and a half ago, and it was valued at just over $1.1 million."

"And has the gift already occurred?" we asked. "Did he already transfer the title to you?"

Jane hesitantly shook her head no. "Wonderful," we both laughed loudly. "You could have lost out on a big tax-saving opportunity if your dad had already gifted the property to you."

Jane suddenly began to panic. She had not even realized there were taxes she had to worry about. After all, she had always been under the impression that she did not have to pay taxes on a gift.

Receiving a Gift Versus Receiving an Inheritance

Although Jane was right that she did not have to pay taxes on a gift she received, but that was not what we were talking about. We were referring to capital gains taxes. You see, if her dad simply gifted the property to Jane, she would receive her dad's basis in the property. Because her dad purchased the property so long ago for only $56,000, he had written off most of the purchase price through his depreciation over the years. After looking at her dad's old tax returns, we noticed that the remaining tax basis on the property was only $16,000. If this property were "gifted" to Jane, her tax basis in the property would also be $16,000. If she were to sell this property down the road for $1.1M, though, she would have a gain of $1,084,000 that she would have to pay capital gains taxes on. This could end up costing her as much as $401,000 in taxes ($1.084M x ~37%).

On the other hand, if the property remained with her dad, and he kept it until he passed away, Jane could inherit the property and get a "basis step-up" to the property's fair market value. In this example, if the fair market value of the property at the time of her dad's death was $1.1M, Jane's tax basis would be $1.1M instead of $16,000. Using the inheritance strategy, if Jane decided to sell the property for $1.1M even just one day after inheriting it, she would pay zero taxes on that transaction.

The difference between her dad gifting her the property today versus waiting to pass it on to her after his death as inheritance meant a potential tax savings of $401,000.

Transfer via Gift	Transfer Via Inheritance
$1,100,000 Sales Price	$1,100,000
($16,000) Carry-Over Basis	($1,100,000) Step-Up Basis
$1,084,000 Total Taxable Gain	$0 Total Taxable Gain
37.0% Tax Rate	37.0% Tax Rate
$401,080 Total Taxes Due	$0 Total Taxes Due

Jane was speechless. This was not something she had ever thought might be an issue. She loved the idea of saving such a large amount in taxes, but she did have her concerns—and not just about herself. She also had to think about her dad's caregiver Patti. If Jane didn't accept her dad's gift before the wedding, she was not sure the property would even pass to her after her dad passed away. If her dad and Patti got married, Patti could ultimately own all her dad's assets as his surviving wife.

Irrevocable Trust

Working with Jane and her family attorney, we recommended setting up an irrevocable trust with retained powers. This was a strategy to help Jane get the best of both worlds by creating some protection for the property transfer, while at the same time minimizing future taxes.

With an irrevocable trust, her dad could move the property into the trust right away while maintaining certain rights. Upon his passing, the property could then be transferred from the trust to Jane, and she would get the step-up basis to fair market value on the date her dad passed away.

A common mistake we see is that as people get older, they try to quickly move assets out of their name and into their kids' names. As you can see in Jane and her dad's situation, this may not always be a good idea. There are times when moving an asset to beneficiaries before one's death could make sense, but at other times, it can be a costly decision.

This can be a tricky decision, especially with respect to real estate. For example, it is possible to use 1031 exchange strategies to permanently defer taxes on your properties. How? Simply die while owning it!

Permanently Tax-Free Gains

As morbid as it may sound, "dying while owning" is actually an advanced strategy commonly used by investors. Let's go over an example.

Let's say you purchased a piece of real estate for $100,000. Several years later, the property has appreciated significantly in value to $300,000, and you are ready to trade up. Rather than selling it outright and losing 15%–37% in taxes, you do a 1031 exchange into a larger property. Let's say you now own a $300,000 property. The $200,000 of gain is deferred for tax purposes, and as such, no income taxes are due until you eventually sell the replacement property or you do another 1031 exchange.

Let's say a few more years go by, and your keen eye for real estate has paid off again—now your property is worth $500,000. You sell that second property and exchange it into a third property worth $500,000. All in all, you have paid zero taxes on your real estate sales and have now deferred $400,000 of capital gains from taxes.

If you were to pass away with this property in your name, your beneficiaries would get a step-up basis as of the date of your death, free from income taxes. Assuming that by the time you pass away, the property is worth $700,000, you and your beneficiaries would receive $600,000 of capital gains completely tax free.

Had you instead cashed out by selling the property or gifting it to your beneficiaries without proper planning, you could have had to pay taxes on the $600,000 of capital gains you had deferred all those years. But if the property remained in your name until your death, neither you nor your beneficiaries would ever have to pay taxes on the $600,000 of capital gains.

Jane realized for the first time that she was responsible for doing whatever she could to preserve and protect the assets her dad had worked so hard for all his life. She now knew there was so much more to building and preserving wealth than she had ever imagined. She finally understood the benefit of having a tax advisor on her team, and for the first time in her life, she felt like she was planning proactively and doing the right things.

What Does All This Mean?

We may call him Uncle Sam, but we all know he is not really our uncle. When given the choice, most of us would rather leave our hard-earned wealth to our family, friends, and preferred charities than to Uncle Sam. We have never met a client who told us Uncle Sam was their intended beneficiary.

Wouldn't it be terrible to spend the last moments of your life regretting that you hadn't planned adequately to help your heirs protect their inheritance from the IRS? Most of us do not like to even think about death, so planning for death is no real picnic, either. However, as you can see from Jane's story, a slight change in her dad's legacy planning can have a huge tax-saving impact. So, however unpleasant a task it may be, make sure to plan accordingly to protect your wealth for your intended beneficiaries.

Getting the IRS to Help Cover Your Real Estate Losses

When you lose money in real estate, call on Uncle Sam to help you shoulder the burden.

— Anonymous

As wonderful as real estate investing can be for wealth building, we have yet to meet a real estate investor who has never lost money. In fact, the two of us have made some not-so-good investment decisions in the past ourselves and have lost our share of money in real estate deals gone sideways.

The silver lining is that we can hopefully take what we've learned and come out the other side as better and more astute investors. What investors forget about are the potential tax benefits available when they lose money on deals.

> ***Real Life:*** *Connie has always been an ambitious woman. After working as an executive in corporate America for over two decades, she stood shoulder to shoulder with some of the most successful men in the world. Connie did not like mistakes and took extra steps to make sure she didn't make them often. So when she started investing in real estate six years ago, she did so only after careful analysis of both the market and her two target properties.*
>
> *It's hard, if not impossible, to predict the future, however. We*

have all had moments when we thought, "If I had only known then what I know now." Let's just say this was Connie's first experience with real estate.

Six years ago, Connie announced to her husband that they were going to invest in real estate. Through her research, she had determined that downtown Las Vegas was going to be a great area to invest in. Everything she had read indicated that the Las Vegas market had been exploding with growth over the past several years. With the proposal of a downtown revitalization program, prices in the area were sure to skyrocket in the coming years. The two properties Connie had under contract were not in the best of neighborhoods, but with the expected revitalization program, Connie felt her money would be safe invested in the two rentals. After all, what could go wrong with rental real estate, right? Actually, it looked like a lot of things could go wrong.

Connie was trying to decide whether or not to hire a management company for her properties. She liked the idea of not having to deal with tenants but cringed at the thought of handing over 8% of her rent in management fees each month. She thought she would test the waters by first listing the properties on Craigslist to see if she could fill the houses herself, and things started out great. Both rentals were snatched up by tenants almost as soon as she listed them online; however, she didn't get very far before her luck ran out.

The tenants who moved into the first rental property never paid rent beyond the initial deposit and first month. From that point on, Connie spent a lot of time and effort each month trying to coax these people into paying her. What she later learned was that these terrible tenants were actually professional scammers. They knew the system and were able to work it to their advantage to stay in a place as long as possible without paying. Not until after almost eight months of zero rental income did the courts finally force eviction on these tenants. To make matters worse, when the scammers finally left, they trashed the house and took whatever fixtures and appliances they could with them. Connie was shocked to find out that they even took the doorknobs off all the doors before smashing in the windows and leaving.

Connie's second rental didn't work out much better. Although *this tenant paid on time, she was a major headache and would call Connie on a weekly basis with complaints about things that needed to be fixed. From leaky plumbing to a broken dishwasher, it seemed to Connie that the repairs list for this unit was constantly growing. After a few months of management, Connie finally threw in the towel and hired a management company. By then, she was more than happy to pay the 8% management fee. In fact, she was happy just to get her life back; it was not easy to work a full-time job and manage her rentals.*

Unfortunately for Connie, her stream of bad luck didn't end there. Over the next several years, the real estate bubble burst, and Las Vegas was one of the hardest hit areas. The drop in home prices led to a drop in rents as well. With the downturn in the economy, the big downtown revitalization project was put on hold indefinitely. Connie's real estate dream had turned into a real estate nightmare. With two rentals that had negative cash flow and negative equity, she gave the properties back to the bank and walked away from her failed investment.

This was not an easy decision for Connie, and she lost quite a bit of money on the deal. Over the years, she had accumulated roughly $40,000 in losses on her tax returns that were considered passive losses. Her CPA explained to her that these losses were being preserved for future use, because her income was too high for the losses to help her at the time. The good thing, her CPA noted, was that she could use the losses to offset any future gains she would get on the sale of the rentals. As it turned out, future gains were the last thing on Connie's mind. She just wanted to get out with as little loss as possible.

Connie initially purchased the properties for a total of $435,000. With outstanding loans of $320,000 and the current market value of her rentals at only $220,000, Connie's only options had been a short sale or foreclosure.

With the help of a friend in the mortgage industry, she was able to negotiate a short sale with the bank on both properties. Connie was extremely pleased to have ended her real estate nightmare with as few bruises as possible—or so she thought until she met with her CPA.

Adding Insult to Injury

Connie had heard from friends about people who had gone through short sale transactions and needed to pay taxes. She just never thought she would be one of them. When Connie met with her CPA the following April, she was disappointed to learn that the 1099 the bank issued her for $320,000 was indeed something she needed to pay taxes on. Her CPA explained that because the bank had relieved her of this debt, it was as if the money had been given to her, and as a result, this was technically income she owed taxes on.

The CPA said that silver lining in all this was that Connie had accumulated losses on the rentals over the previous several years, and those losses would help reduce her taxes in the future. The only caveat was that the losses were capital losses.

Capital losses are not like ordinary losses that you can use to offset your income without limitations. On the contrary, capital losses can only offset capital gains, and if there are excess losses, you can take only $3,000 each year on your tax return. The rest needs to be carried forward into future years.

Therefore, Connie ended up with a large tax bill thanks to the bank's 1099 as well as a significant amount of capital losses she could offset with only $3,000 on her tax return. Although she was glad the rest of the losses would roll forward and not be disallowed or disappear, she wished she were able to use them right away to offset the 1099 income.

To Connie, this felt like adding insult to injury. It was bad enough that she had lost so much money on her real estate deals, but it seemed like the IRS was kicking her on her way down. Something didn't seem right.

Connie called up her friend Clarice, who had recently gone through a similar ordeal. After hearing that Clarice's CPA had been able to help her avoid taxes, Connie decided to get a second opinion on her own situation.

Speaking with Connie for the first time was almost exactly like the first time we spoke with her friend Clarice. In fact, their situations were almost identical. Even though they were working with two different tax advisors, those advisors had made the same unfortunate mistake—one we see very often with real estate losses.

Getting a 1099 Doesn't Always Mean You Need to Pay Taxes

The big mistake Connie's tax preparer had made involved the short sale transaction. He was correct in stating that Connie may have had to pay taxes on the 1099 income from the bank. However, it isn't just a straightforward matter of entering that amount on the tax forms and letting the software decide the tax. In fact, if dealt with correctly, that income could have actually worked to Connie's advantage. How can you go from taxable income of $320,000 to a tax advantage, you ask? Let's break down Connie's situation one step at a time to see how her tax return should have been done.

Cancellation of Debt Income

$320,000 Debt Outstanding

($220,000) Fair Market Value

$100,000 Cancellation of Debt Income

The first step was to calculate how much of the $320,000 of discharged debt was actually taxable for Connie. The 1099 from the bank was inaccurate in showing that the entire outstanding debt amount was taxable. Although the outstanding loan balances totaled $320,000 just before the short sale, the entire amount was not taxable for Connie. The fair market value of the properties—which they actually sold for—can be used to reduce the taxable income. So in Connie's case, only $100,000 of the $320,000 of 1099 income was taxable (i.e., only $100,000 of the loan balances were "forgiven").

This was very important to show on Connie's tax return, because it immediately moved $220,000 from the taxable bucket into the tax-free bucket.

Don't Forget Your Losses

The next step is to look at what losses, if any, Connie incurred as a result of this transaction. To determine this, we looked at the difference between what the properties sold for (i.e., their fair market value) and Connie's cost basis in the properties. To keep things simple for illustration purposes here, we will assume Connie took no depreciation on the two rentals, so her basis was the properties' initial purchase price: $435,000.

$220,000 Sales Price

($435,000) Cost Basis

($215,000) Ordinary Loss

As you can see, Connie had a loss of $215,000, according to this calculation. But here is where the capital loss mistake commonly occurs. Connie's tax preparer, like quite a few others we've seen, treated this $215,000 as a capital loss instead of an ordinary loss. As a result, Connie was not able to use the loss to offset her cancellation of debt income.

The truth is that losses on rental properties are ordinary losses, not capital losses. Because the loss on the sale of rental properties is an ordinary loss, there is no limit to how much can be used each year to offset taxes. In Connie's example, she was legitimately able to use her loss on the sale of the properties to offset the cancellation of debt income.

$100,000 Cancellation of Debt Income

($215,000) Ordinary Loss

($115,000) Net Ordinary Loss

Connie was able to use all her real estate losses in one year and completely wipe out the 1099 income from the bank on the short sale transactions. In addition, remember the $40,000 in losses she had accumulated over the years on her rentals? Well, that was also considered an ordinary loss she could use in the same year the properties were short sold. All in all, Connie ended up with $155,000 of additional losses after wiping out her 1099 income.

$100,000 Cancellation of Debt Income

($215,000) Ordinary Loss

($40,000) Passive Loss from Prior Year

($155,000) Net Ordinary Loss

Coming Out Ahead

The good news was that she would be able to use the ordinary losses to offset her W-2 income. At her federal and state tax rate of 38%, this meant she would receive a tax refund of $58,900. So rather than paying taxes of $121,600 ($320,000 x 38%), she was getting a $58,900 refund. That is $173,660 in tax savings!

Why Is This Mistake Made So Often?

So why exactly did her tax preparer file the original return incorrectly? This is actually a fairly common mistake and an easy one to make. Tax preparers may mistakenly show the loss on the sale of a rental property as capital loss because under IRS rules, a gain on the sale of a rental property is considered capital gain. So, if you bought a property for $100,000 and sold it a few years later for $150,000, the $50,000 difference is considered a capital gain and is therefore subject to lower capital gains taxes. This is actually a tax benefit available to real estate investors. However, because the gain on the sale of a rental property is a capital gain, some tax preparers may incorrectly treat a loss in this situation as a capital loss. If you think about it, it makes sense: when you sell a rental for a gain, it is a capital gain, and if you sell it for a loss, it is a capital loss, right?

Well, if you answered yes, you would have made the same mistake Connie's tax preparer made. The beauty of the tax world is in the loopholes. The truth is that when you sell a property for a gain, it is indeed a capital gain, and you may be able to pay less tax using the lower tax rates. However, when you sell a rental property at a loss, the loss is actually considered an ordinary loss. An ordinary loss is better than a capital loss for two reasons:

1. With an ordinary loss, there is no annual limit on how much can be used to offset your income.

2. You can use an ordinary loss to offset your ordinary income, which is generally taxed at a higher rate.

So yes, under IRS rules, real estate investors can actually get the best of both worlds:

- If you sell a long-term rental for a gain, you pay less taxes at the long-term capital gains tax rates.

- Conversely, if you sell a long-term rental at a loss, you get to pay fewer taxes because the losses are considered ordinary.

If you are confused, don't worry. This strange benefit confuses most people, including tax preparers. Every year, we see a handful of investors fall victim to this common yet costly mistake. It's important to note that this treatment is not just for short sales or foreclosures. The capital gain and ordinary loss treatment on rental properties applies to all rental transactions. So if you bought a property and sold it for a loss, you are probably looking at a big write-off on your taxes in the year you sold the property.

If you sold rentals at a loss within the last few years and now suspect those losses were not written off correctly, it doesn't hurt to get a second opinion. What's the worst that can happen?

As for Connie, believe it or not, she didn't give up on real estate. She was determined to learn from her mistakes and do better the next time. In fact, with the current depressed real estate market, she was already doing research for her next deal. This was all a secret to her husband, though. Even though she was ready to make her next move in real estate, she felt her husband might need a little more recovery time. Connie's plan was to surprise her husband with the big $58,900 tax refund check and maybe announce her new investment plans that same day. Ha, ha!

What Does All This Mean?

Yes, it seems strange that on the sale of a rental property, you can get capital gains at a lower tax rate and higher deductions when you lose money at ordinary income rates. As investors, do we really care why this loophole exists? No, of course not! All we care is that we can use the loophole to our advantage. Losing money in real estate is painful enough; make sure to lessen that pain by capturing and maximizing all the tax benefits that go along with it.

Remember, don't fall into the common mistake of assuming the 1099s issued by a bank are correct. We all know that banks, like everyone else, can make mistakes. If you are ever unsure whether your taxes are being done correctly, take the time to get a second opinion!

Explosive Tax Landmine for Fix and Flippers

The blame for the maddening complications of the federal tax system goes to the people with the most money.

— Nicholas Von Hoffman

Did you know that the way rental income is taxed is significantly different from how fix-and-flip profit is taxed? And did you know that the deductions and depreciations for rentals and flips might also differ? Because the taxation of rentals is not the same as for flips, many investors who switch from being landlords to being flippers can unexpectedly get caught in an bind when tax time comes.

> **Real Life:** *Francisco is what you would call a "serial entrepreneur." Meeting with him is always fun, because he is usually up to some new and exciting business venture. Francisco is always thinking of clever ways to save money and make money at the same time.*
>
> *For example, one time he told us he felt he was paying his rehab crew too much money to purchase plants for his backyard renovations. Rather than price shopping for the plants, he was going to purchase his own nursery to grow plants and then sell them to other rehabbers. Over the years, we have seen some of Francisco's successful (and not so successful) business ventures in the real estate realm. Not*

only is he passionate about real estate investing, but he is also passionate about pretty much everything related to real estate investing.
From landscaping to construction to investor relations, this man lives,
breathes, and dreams real estate.

But it wasn't always this way for Francisco. When we first met
him, he was not at all the real estate mogul he is today. In fact, he was
a financial planner who focused on helping his clients invest their
money in the stock market. We will never forget our first meeting
with him, at a pastrami sandwich shop in the heart of downtown
Los Angeles.

What surprised us was that when we got to the restaurant just
before lunchtime on a Tuesday, the place was pretty much empty.
Thinking that this restaurant was probably on the verge of closing
down, we were shocked when Francisco proclaimed that the shop was
the "best investment decision" he had ever made. He confirmed that
the restaurant was not working out very well and was indeed on
the verge of closing down, but for Francisco, the real gem was the
real estate the sandwich shop was on. You see, Francisco owned the
property that housed the sandwich shop. With the recent downtown
revival, he was getting offers left and right from people who wanted
to purchase the property. In fact, Francisco estimated that he could
probably make more money on the sale of the building than he had
in all five years of owning it.

Now there was a potential tax issue related to the gain he would
make from selling the building. After factoring in the property's original purchase price and all the improvements he had made over the
years, Francisco was looking at a pretty significant gain of $900,000
on the sale. Had he sold the property outright and kept the cash, his
estimated tax liability in total would have been close to $342,000.
Rather than keeping the cash, Francisco invested all his windfall into
more real estate.

This was great news tax-wise, because we could help Francisco
use a 1031 exchange strategy to defer the taxes of $342,000 on that
$900,000 tax gain. We connected him with an exchange intermedi-
ary company that facilitated the transaction, and for a few thousand
dollars, he was able to save a significant amount in taxes.

What we didn't know at the time was that this was the start of

Francisco's love affair with real estate. Actually, love affair may not even be the best way to describe it. It was more like an addiction. You see, after Francisco sold the sandwich shop building, he used the money to buy an apartment complex. Shortly after that, he got out of the stock market altogether and even went so far as to close down the financial planning firm he owned.

Francisco was now focusing full-time on real estate. He wasted no time at all in obtaining his real estate license, and he subsequently began a fix-and-flip business. After years of experience in the financial planning business, raising money always came easily to Francisco. Even though he had closed down his firm, he still had a book full of clients with whom he kept in very close contact, and they trusted him to place their money into various deals.

Before long, Francisco was in charge of a pretty decent-sized real estate empire. One of his investment strategies was to purchase, rehab, and sell single-family homes. But Francisco didn't sell these homes to just anyone. Mostly, he sold them to his investor clients. With buyers already lining up to purchase his properties, his fix-and-flip business grew exponentially.

His real estate business was flourishing, his clients were happy, and money was coming in. The only bad news for Francisco seemed to be the potential tax hit he might take when the IRS finally took its share of his fix-and-flip profit.

The IRS shows no mercy, of course, and what people do not know is that the IRS treats fixing and flipping as an active business. This means it's very different from rental real estate. The following are some key differences between rentals and fix and flips:

1. Fix and flip is generally considered active income and is subject to payroll or self-employment taxes of up to 15%. Rentals, on the other hand, are never subject to this additional tax.

2. Fix-and-flip properties are not eligible for capital gains tax and are instead taxed at the higher ordinary income tax rates.

3. Fix-and-flip properties are not generally eligible for long-term capital gains tax rates, regardless of how long you own the flip property before selling it.

4. Fix-and-flip properties are generally treated as inventory and are not eligible for the same depreciation tax write-off as rental properties.

5. With a fix-and-flip property, you cannot write off the purchase price of the property until the year it is sold.

All five of these points can be very detrimental to a flipper's bottom line. Of course, there are strategies for getting around some of these nasty tax regulations.

Of the five points just listed, the fifth one catches most investors off guard. Let's take Francisco, for example. In the year Francisco started his fix-and-flip business, he purchased five properties and flipped them for a profit of $300,000. Later that same year, he used that $300,000 profit to purchase three more properties to flip. Because the entire $300,000 profit was used to buy more real estate, Francisco thought he would pay zero income taxes on that money.

Francisco's Logic

$500,000 Gross Sale Price of Flips

($200,000) Cost of Flip Properties Sold

$300,000 Net Profit from Flips Sold

($300,000) Purchase of Additional Flips

$0 Taxable Income

Although this seemed like a wonderful idea in Francisco's mind, unfortunately, it does not work in the real world under the U.S. tax code. You see, in a fix-and-flip business, you generally cannot take a write-off for the purchase of a property until that property is sold. So, rather than writing off the purchase price of a property in the same year you buy it, you must wait to write that cost off in the year that it is ultimately sold.

Now we know this seems unfair. Most people feel that if they spent the money that year, they must surely be able to write it off that same year. After all, buying a flip property is a business expense, isn't it?

Unfortunately, the IRS considers the flip property "inventory" and not a business deduction like mortgage interest on a rental property. Therefore, as with any other business, inventory you purchase is deducted on the tax return in the same year it is sold. If you purchased and sold a property in the same year, you're in luck. If not, you have to hang on to that inventory until a later year when the property is sold.

Let's look at a car dealership, for example. If the dealership owner purchases $1M worth of cars at the beginning of the year, he cannot take a $1M tax deduction that year. Instead, this $1M of inventory is entered into the company's books, and the cost of each car is written off at the time that car is sold.

This is the same for a fix-and-flip business. So in Francisco's example, in his first year, he purchased five properties and flipped them for a profit of $300,000. Later that year, he used that $300,000 profit to buy three more properties to flip. Even though the entire $300,000 profit was used to purchase that new real estate, the bottom line is that Francisco made $300,000 in profit on his flips, and that amount could be subject to IRS income tax.

The Tax World

Year 1

$500,000 Gross Sale Price of Flips

($200,000) Cost of Flip Properties Sold

$300,000 Net Profit from Flips Sold (Taxable Income)

The good news is that the following year, when those three properties are sold, the $300,000 in inventory can be used to reduce Francisco's taxable income that year. For example, if in his second year, the three properties sold for $400,000, his total taxable income in that year would be only $100,000.

Year 2

$400,000 Gross Sale Price of Flips

($300,000) Cost of Flip Properties Sold

$100,000 Taxable Income

As you can see, this can create a big issue for Francisco. Because he anticipated that he would be paying zero taxes on his flip profit, Francisco reinvested his entire $300,000 profit into more flip properties. As a result, he was tight on cash when the time came to pay the IRS its share in taxes.

Thankfully for Francisco, we were able to use cost segregation to accelerate the depreciation on his apartment building and some of his other rentals to offset a big chunk of his taxes on the flip profits. He was also fortunate to have some other cash set aside to fund retirement accounts, which helped bring down the taxes on the $300,000 income.

However, the reality is that every taxpayer's profit is different, and not everyone is as lucky as Francisco. We often see flippers who do not have other rental properties to offset their unexpected tax bills. Sometimes a flipper may not even realize how much profit they made during the year, because all that money went directly into the next deal. Tying up all your cash by reinvesting it into more deals without first considering your tax consequences can be a giant mistake.

So be sure to strategize with your tax advisor to determine ways of minimizing that tax bite so you can protect yourself from any unexpected surprises.

What Does All This Mean?

Clearly, not all real estate transactions are equal with regard to taxation. Investors who flip and those who own rental properties are subject to completely different rules. With the correct strategies, however, you can structure your deals so the tax benefits of your rentals may be used to offset the tax burden of your flip profits.

Remember, the IRS is one of the few agencies that can garnish your wages and levy assets, so you do not want to fall short of paying your due. Before reinvesting all your profits into a new deal, find out how much you need to set aside to cover the taxes any flip properties sold that year.

Guilty Until Proven Innocent

You're guilty until proven innocent. Perception is reality, that's the way that it is in this world.

— Chris Webber

A common question we get is "What are my odds of being audited?" The truth is, no one knows. The IRS has never released its secret internal formula for determining exactly whom and which tax returns to audit. However, it is widely believed that if a taxpayer is audited and significant discrepancies are identified, that taxpayer's chances of being audited again in the future are extremely high.

Although inarguably an unpleasant experience, being audited does not necessarily need to be painful. There are many things we can do on a daily basis as taxpayers to protect ourselves from audit potential and minimize the pain an audit might bring.

> **Real Life:** *There was always so much to do after being away from home for a few weeks. From unpacking bags to doing the laundry and heading out for groceries, Judy had been busy ever since she had returned from her real estate conference in Arizona two days ago. Being back in Maine and the snow, she really missed the warm sunshine of the desert and most of all, her daughter Darla.*
>
> *Getting into real estate investing was one of the best decisions*

151

Judy and her late husband had ever made. Now that she was retired, Judy received some pension and social security income, but the money from the rentals was a significant source of income that had allowed her to maintain her preferred lifestyle in retirement. Judy was well aware of the benefits investing had afforded her, and this is why she was so happy to have convinced Darla to get into real estate as well by having Darla help her with some of her existing properties. Judy deeply believed in teaching her kids to fish themselves rather than just feeding them the fish she had caught.

Two days after getting home, Judy finally started sorting through her mail. She smiled when she saw the rent checks from her eight rental property tenants that came in on time. But partway through her stack of mail, Judy saw a thick envelope with the words "important document" stamped on the front in red. She glanced at the sender and panicked.

Judy tore open the envelope. Her hands shook as she took out the letter and read the words she hoped she would never have to see again:

Dear Judy,

Your federal return for the period shown above was selected for examination.

Judy knew what this meant. She and her late husband had been audited before, almost a decade ago, and it had been a horrible experience. Back then, she sold Mary Kay cosmetics on the side and made a small amount of income. The IRS did not like the expenses she had claimed for her cosmetics work. In the end, Judy lost the fight and ended up needing to pay the IRS for back taxes. It was such a bad and stressful experience that she vowed to never deal with the IRS again. This time, she would have her CPAs represent her, and this time, she would win—or at least she hoped so.

The information on the pages that came with the audit notice didn't make any sense to her. It included references to tax form numbers, information on whom to call, and explanations of taxpayer rights.

Having been through an audit before, Judy knew better than to believe in these "taxpayer rights." She felt there was no such thing.

Her audit experience had taught her the truth about the IRS and the amount of power they really had over the average taxpayer.

Unlike the U.S. criminal court system, which deems a person innocent until proven guilty, the IRS has a completely different viewpoint: the taxpayer is guilty until proven innocent.

Contrary to popular belief, it is the taxpayer who needs to prove their case in the event of an audit, not the IRS. If the IRS agent asks you to prove your deductions, and you don't have your receipts in order, they can disallow your deduction. Unless you take the matter to court to dispute it, disallowed deduction and expense issues usually end with you writing a check to the IRS.

Before getting audited, Judy was never really worried about her taxes and didn't stress when tax day rolled around. When getting her tax documents together, she didn't give a second thought to whether or not she could write something off. Judy had always thought that the odds were in her favor. Like a lot of taxpayers, when something came into question, Judy's position had always been "How could the IRS prove that this was not a business expense?"

As tax advisors, we frequently meet with taxpayers who ask, "If I take a deduction for a trip that I claim is a business trip, how can the IRS prove that it wasn't?" The short answer is that the IRS can't and doesn't need to! We taxpayers must prove that our trip was a business trip and eligible as a tax deduction.

Judy learned this the hard way. Back when Judy was doing cosmetics sales, it was more of a hobby than a business. Mary Kay was a network marketing business built on social interactions, and naturally, Judy often hosted parties for her girlfriends to try on makeup and maybe drink a little wine, in hopes of selling some products. She wasn't the best at keeping all her receipts, but then again, she didn't know she was required to do so. She was mostly enjoying the social aspects of the job and not so much the business side. Judy, like a lot of taxpayers, was under the impression that bank statements and credit card statements were enough for an audit.

When the auditor looked through her books, they did start with her bank statements, but they didn't stop there. They wanted Judy to produce receipts for every single item she had listed as a deduction on her return. The auditor also indicated that for any items to be tax deductible, Judy must prove that they were business related.

This all came as a complete surprise to Judy, and she learned in those stressful months that essentially, the IRS assumes all expenses are non-business related and nondeductible unless you can prove otherwise. The IRS wanted documents confirming that business was conducted during each and every party before she could write off her expenses. Almost two years had passed since she had incurred those business expenses, so looking over all the documents, Judy honestly wasn't sure anymore what each and every expense was.

No matter what she said or did, the IRS denied her expenses, claiming that she just didn't have enough proof. After months and months of going back and forth, Judy eventually surrendered and wrote an $8,000 check to the government. At that point, she didn't care if she won; she just wanted the audit to be over.

Years later, when Judy started real estate investing, she hired us to be her CPAs because we specialized in working with investors like her. In our first meeting together, Judy told us about her audit nightmare and indicated that from now on, she wanted to be 100% audit proof while still maximizing her tax deductions. She had no intentions of going through that misery again.

Audit Proof

The truth is that there is no such thing as being 100% audit proof, and anyone who tells you otherwise is lying. What you can do, however, is protect yourself with the 3-Layer Audit Protection Plan. This plan is designed to ensure that you minimize your audit risk and, if you do get audited, that you maximize your chance of winning against the IRS.

Layer 1: Minimize Audit Risk

The best way to resolve an IRS audit is to never get selected in the first place. Many people don't know that there are things each of us can do to proactively minimize our audit risk. Certain factors stand out to the IRS as "red flags" and make you much more likely to be selected over someone else. By avoiding these common red flags, you can lower your chances of being audited.

Use Legal Entities

If you have an active real estate business with a lot of losses, it may make sense to operate as a legal entity. Partnerships and S corporations are audited fifteen to seventeen times less often than are sole proprietorships, though no one knows for certain why this is. If we had to guess, we would say it's because finding tax revenue with sole proprietors is easier for the IRS, because they are usually smaller or newer businesses, and a new business owner is more likely to have poor financial records or lost receipts than a large established business operating as a corporation or partnership would.

Knowing this, there are easy things you can do to significantly reduce your audit risk. For example, if you are a real estate agent getting paid in commission income via a 1099, consider forming a business entity to earn that income rather than earning it in your name as a sole proprietor. This small change alone could significantly lessen your chances of being audited.

Fly Under the Radar

You can keep your audit risk low by flying under the radar, so to speak. The IRS has a set of algorithms in its secret "vault." Although these exact formulas are closely guarded, they can essentially calculate national and industry averages that allow the IRS to flag tax returns with numbers outside of those norms. The system is also set up to flag certain tax returns that indicate out-of-the-ordinary spending habits with respect to income-to-expense ratios.

For example, based on these industry averages, an American making $100,000 per year in income may be expected to pay between $20,000 and $30,000 each year in mortgage interest for their primary home. If the IRS processes a return for someone who earns $100,000 but spends $120,000 on mortgage interest, that person would have a higher audit risk, because the system would flag that this person is living off more money than they are showing on their tax returns. It would also raise a red flag because their annual mortgage interest is suspiciously higher than the average for that income level.

Because every taxpayer is different, it is definitely possible that your tax return could include items that shift you outside the normal range. However, this alone does not mean you are guaranteed to be audited; it simply means your chances of being audited are higher. This also doesn't mean that you should only reflect national averages on your tax return or plan your finances around these averages. As long as you have adequate documentation to support your tax write-offs, you shouldn't lose any sleep over this.

Layer 2: Accuracy and Matching

Do you remember when tax returns were prepared by hand? Well, that rarely happens these days, and that is a good thing. One way to guarantee that you receive an IRS notice is to have incorrect calculations in your tax returns, because this is something the IRS computer will catch automatically. If you happen to be preparing your own tax returns, don't do them by hand! Spend the $30 to invest in tax preparation software to ensure the calculations are correct.

Report Everything You Have, Even If It's Not Taxable

Another way to protect yourself from the IRS's notice is to make sure your tax return amounts match what the IRS has on its end. This means your wages and interest income from your W-2 and 1099s match what your bank and employer have reported to the IRS. Before you even file your returns, the IRS knows roughly what your income and expenses are based on the wages your employer reported, the mortgage interest paid on your home your lender reported, the interest income reported by your bank, and any rental income your property manager reported.

Even if you receive a tax document that you know is for a transaction that is not taxable, make sure to send it to your tax advisor so they can disclose it correctly on your returns. For example, if you receive a 1099 on the sale of your primary home that you know is not taxable, bring it to your CPA. Otherwise. you might get a nasty letter from the IRS for not reporting the sale correctly.

Be Specific

What investors who don't have good bookkeeping habits often do is create an expense account called "other" or "miscellaneous" and lump all their deductions under this account. Another common mistake is that rather than classifying expenses into the right categories, taxpayers simply take the entire year's worth of expenses on their credit card and deduct that total as "credit card expenses" on their tax return.

Both of these are big flags for an IRS auditor, because they suspect you have buried items in these "miscellaneous" expense accounts. Instead, break the expenses out into the correct categories (e.g., travel, marketing, dues). This way, the IRS can see that you have itemized your expenses for more accurate reporting. It is okay to have an account such as "other expenses," because from time to time, we do have miscellaneous costs of $5 here and $20 there that may not make sense to break out. Keeping these "other" and "miscellaneous" expenses small and reasonable can go a long way in keeping your audit risk low.

Layer 3: Documentation Support

Like most real estate investors, and most taxpayers for that matter, Judy doesn't like to spend time on paperwork. She would much rather sit in the sun or read a good book. Nevertheless, Judy's traumatic audit experience taught her that keeping good records is the key to winning against the IRS.

Separate Bank Accounts

During an audit, the IRS will very likely want to see your bank statements. If you don't have separate bank accounts for your personal and real estate activities, this can be problematic. Commingling personal and business activities makes it a lot harder for you to prove that certain items are business related and not personal. Therefore, having separate accounts can help you limit what the IRS can see. For example, let's say you operated your wholesale real estate business in an S corporation, but you used one bank account for both personal and S corporation transactions. If your S corporation is ever audited, you will need to send the IRS bank statements showing activity for both personal and business items. By giving them this information, you are subjecting your personal tax return to an audit as well. Keeping different bank accounts for your personal and your business activities helps with your documentation and minimizes other audit possibilities.

Receipts or No Receipts

Poor record keeping is common for most investors. Even as CPAs, we're sometimes guilty of losing receipts or forgetting about small expenses. At the moment money is spent, it may not seem like a big deal, but when tax time comes, it can prove to be a pain. In the event of an audit, receipts are our insurance policy. That's right, bank statements alone are not enough; the

IRS wants to see actual receipts. The reasoning behind this is that the bank statements may not necessarily show what the money was spent on. For example, if you spent $100 at Costco to buy paper and pens for your office, the bank statement simply shows $100 paid to Costco. You can't tell from that statement what specifically you spent the money on. Remember, the IRS assumes you are guilty until proven innocent, so it will assume that this $100 was used to buy groceries unless you can prove—typically, and ideally, with receipts—that it was in fact used for office supplies.

Here is the good news: all you need to do as a taxpayer is keep your receipts. There is no need to organize them unless you get audited. So what you can do is keep a folder or envelope for your receipts each month and simply file them away somewhere. The IRS will also accept receipts in electronic format. We all hate those actual receipts, tiny pieces of paper that get crumpled up in your purse or your pocket and become unreadable after a few weeks. What we do is take a picture with our phone of every receipt as we get it and then throw the actual paper receipt away. Then, once a month, we pull those pictures off our phone and file them away in a folder (e.g., "March receipts"). If we ever need any of those receipts, we can just go to that folder, where they will already be sorted by date and time.

Other Documentation

In reality, receipts are not the only things you need to prove your tax deductions. If you made non-cash charitable donations, for example, you may not get receipts for those donated items. This is a great example of how photographs can be good documentation. Taking a picture of your donated items is an easy way to support your charitable donation claims. Pictures are also useful for visits to look at investment properties. For example, if you traveled to Las Vegas to address some issues with your rental there, taking a picture of the broken lawn sprinkler you drove all the way out there to fix for is an effective way to show you were actually there.

Activity logs such as mileage logs, calendars, and phone records are also great documentation that can help you prove your case in an IRS audit.

Judy has been following our advice for the past several years with regard to keeping good records and documenting her paperwork. It was initially very hard for her to take the extra steps to get organized, but over time, she made it a habit and built the steps into her system. Now she always makes sure she has her debit cards for her personal and business accounts with her wherever she goes so she can put each charge on the correct card. Judy also has an envelope for each month in which she keeps all her receipts, with handwritten notes indicating what they were for. Every time Judy receives a document in the mail that says "tax document," she puts it in a folder to be reviewed for her tax returns that year. Once Judy got her system in place, good record keeping became second nature to her and is no longer a big hassle she dreads.

Representation or No Representation?

If you are ever notified that your returns have been selected for an audit, you can choose whether you want to represent yourself or have your tax advisor represent you. The route you take should depend on the complexity of the issues, your budget, and your knowledge of the tax code. Remember, you must provide proof of your tax deductions, not your tax preparer. So having someone represent you doesn't mean they will produce all the necessary receipts for you. That's still something you must do on your own. Having professional representation during an audit does have some benefits over representing yourself, though.

First, tax advisors generally have more experience. When dealing with the auditor, they would likely understand better than you why a certain question is being asked and what the IRS is after. For example, one of the items the IRS requested in Judy's audit related to her education expenses. The IRS wanted a description of each class. By having professional representation, Judy was able to provide these descriptions using the correct language to support why she needed to take the courses for her investing business.

Second, your professional representation acts as a kind of buffer. If you are sitting across from an auditor and are asked a question, odds are you must respond to that question on the spot. And worse, you may not even know the best or "correct" answer to give. We always try to deal with auditors directly and remove our client from these meetings. This way, we can serve as a buffer and can buy some time by saying we need to request information from the client before responding. This gives you more time to gather data and organize a response in your favor.

As much as Judy hated the thought of her upcoming audit, she felt calm and confident knowing she was ready and well equipped this time to face the IRS. This time around, she was ready! She was ecstatic to learn that thanks to her diligent record keeping, the audit was an open-and-shut case that closed in less than three weeks with no additional money due to the IRS.

What Does All This Mean?

As hard as it is to accept, the truth is that in our U.S. tax system, you are presumed guilty until proven innocent. With the burden of proof on us tax-payers, an IRS audit can be a time-consuming and costly ordeal. Let's face it, even if you ultimately "win" an audit, does anyone ever get excited about receiving an audit notification letter? Just the thought of an audit can put a knot in anyone's stomach—even if you have been extremely conservative and accurate on your taxes.

In certain cases, disclosing as much information as possible to preemptively answer any potential IRS questions may be a good idea. Other times, disclosing as little information as necessary to avoid IRS questioning would be more prudent. For real estate investors, a great lesson to take away from Judy's story is to practice good record keeping habits and make documentation part of your investing system. And in the unlikely event of an audit, consider having audit representation to increase your chances of success.

Although there is no guaranteed way to audit proof a tax return, taking some simple steps to minimize your audit risk makes good sense.

CONCLUSION

Putting it All Together

It's not how much money you make, but how much money you keep, how hard it works for you, and how many generations you keep it for.

— Robert T. Kiyosaki

It may sound shocking to hear that the average American pays more money in taxes than they spend on food, clothing, and shelter combined, but unfortunately, that is the reality. With the average person losing 35% to 50% of their income to various types of taxes each year, the tax changes in recent years have made it even tougher for middle- and higher-income Americans to keep more of their hard-earned money.

A large percentage of the population is working harder and harder yet receiving less in return for their efforts. With rising prices, higher taxes, and stagnant pay, the middle-class dream has slowly turned into a nightmare. The fantasy of retiring at an early age to relax on the beach has been replaced by a seemingly infinite number of additional working years.

We meet with clients all the time who desperately want to invest in real estate but never feel they have sufficient money to get started. What people don't realize is that one of the first places to start looking for extra money is in their own pocket. As author Randy Thurman said, "A penny saved is worth two pennies earned… after taxes."

In fact, with the leverage available to real estate investors, a penny saved can be used as a down payment on an investment property worth five

163

pennies. Okay, five pennies may not sound like much, but what if you were able to get an additional $5,000 per year in tax savings? This means that in a two-year period, you could save $10,000 in taxes. Using that as a down payment means you could purchase a rental property worth $50,000 every two years.

So just how exactly do you start on this path to saving taxes? The answer is simple: proactive tax planning.

What Is Proactive Tax Planning?

Tax planning is a proactive way of saving on taxes. Getting together with your tax advisor and creating a solid strategy for putting money back into your pocket rather than handing it over to the government is a good way to accomplish this. For the real estate investor, here are some good times to do proactive tax planning:

- Before you purchase a property
- Before you sell a property
- Before starting a new real estate venture
- Before entering into a partnership or joint venture with others
- Before making any major investments
- Before making any major improvements

It is important to note that proactive tax planning doesn't apply just to real estate transactions. It should also be used for business transactions and plain old life changes. Here are some additional examples of when to engage in proactive tax planning:

- Before you purchase, sell, or expand a business
- Before any major life change, such as marriage, kids, divorce, or college
- Before any job change
- Before retirement
- When a death occurs in the family
- Before purchasing or selling your primary home
- Before going on vacation (see Chapter on deducting your vacation)

The key word in this list is "before." Proactive tax planning means consulting your tax advisor before any of these important transactions are done or decisions made. For example, before you purchase your next investment property, get advice on how to hold the title to that property, what entity to buy it in, and what the best sources of money are to purchase it.

What if you are selling a property? For example, if you expect to sell a property for a $100,000 gain, doing some proactive planning could lead you to use a 1031 exchange to defer the taxes or another offset strategy to wipe out the tax. On the other hand, if you are just now telling your CPA about the $100,000 gain you made on the property you sold last year, there is probably less you can do to minimize your taxes.

If your fix-and-flip business has been going well for the first part of the year, proactive tax planning can inform you of ways to minimize taxes, such as setting up retirement accounts or shifting income to your kids. If you wait until the year is over to talk to your advisor about all that profit, odds are it will be too late for you to apply any of these strategies.

If you plan to leave your job soon, a proactive meeting with your tax advisor can teach you strategic ways of receiving your severance or other payouts. It may also reveal ways you can move your existing retirement money into real estate deals in a tax-free manner.

What Are the Steps?

The word taxes can conjure up very unpleasant feelings. Most people avoid talking about taxes like the plague. Some may even feel that discussing taxes is bad luck, fearing that doing so may somehow prompt the IRS to come knocking. The truth is, taxes aren't all that bad if you know how to manage your finances. Believe it or not, tax planning does not need to be time consuming or intimidating. You do not need to spend hours and hours learning the tax code or memorizing the jargon. Leave that to your tax advisors. Tax planning can actually be quite fun and enjoyable, especially if spending a few hours on it can result in thousands of dollars in savings, right?

So what does proactive tax planning entail, and what are the steps to take?

Step 1: Know where you are today.

Organizing your finances so that you have a fairly good idea where you stand financially is important. How much income are you making? What kind of returns are your investments generating? How much debt do you have? And what are your goals?

Step 2: Get together with the professionals.

Once you know where you stand financially, make an appointment to meet with your tax advisor. During your meeting, be prepared to share how your year has been so far and what other business, investment, or life changes you expect to have going forward. Based on just this casual conversation, your tax advisor should be able to identify opportunities and strategies that can help you minimize taxes.

Step 3: Get a plan in place.

You should leave your meeting with your tax advisor with a set of recommendations and ideas to consider that may help you reduce your taxes and improve your financial well-being. After you decide which of these you will implement, you will be ready to move on to the next step.

Step 4: Implement your plan.

A great plan is useless unless it is put into action. Once you know what you need to do, it's time to actually start doing it. If one of your recommended strategies is to decrease your withholdings at work, immediately request the paperwork to do so. If another recommendation is to form a corporation for your real estate, contact the proper professionals to accomplish this.

Step 5: Review and renew your strategies.

Just as life changes from day to day, so can your tax strategies. A plan your tax advisor recommended in January, when you thought you would be keeping that rental forever, would need to change if in June, you decided to sell it while the market was hot. And a plan your advisor suggested for last year may not be the best strategy for this year. So, as your investments and goals change, be sure to keep your tax advisor updated so they can help you adjust your tax planning as appropriate.

Who Should Do Proactive Tax Planning?

Believe it or not, proactive tax planning is not just for rich people. That is probably one of the most common myths we hear. Yes, the wealthy do usually have their tax advisor on speed dial, and they don't make buy or sell decisions without first consulting their advisor, but that definitely does not mean proactive tax planning is only for those with lots of money.

At the same time, we are not saying that everyone needs proactive tax planning. In fact, here are some examples of people who should not do tax planning:

- No Investments: If you do not have any investments yet, proactive planning may not be for you. Do not spend all your money on accounting and legal fees until you are making money in real estate or business or from other investments.

- No Money: If you do not have any money, then proactive planning is not for you. I have met tons of people who have been advised to use credit cards or even liquidate their retirement money just to pay for tax and legal advice. That is the worst thing anyone can do. Only invest in proactive tax planning if you have the money to do so.

- No Taxes: This may be obvious, but if you do not have a tax liability, then proactive tax planning may not be for you. Now we're not talking about getting a refund each year because you withheld a lot of taxes. We mean those individuals who truly do not have any tax liability at all. If your tax rate is already at zero, you probably do not need any tax advice.

For the rest of us, proactive tax planning can be extremely helpful. In fact, just from reading this book, you should already be able to see how tax strategies can be effectively used by ordinary, everyday investors. You don't need to be Donald Trump to write off your travel costs. You don't need to be Bill Gates to pay your kids and take a write-off. You don't need to be Warren Buffett to claim a home office deduction. These strategies are easily applicable to average investors like you.

To do proactive tax planning, will you need to do some work yourself? Probably a little. Does proactive planning cost money? Probably yes. If you had the opportunity to pay $3,000 for tax planning and it saved you $5,000 in taxes, would that be a good investment? What if those strategies saved you $5,000 in taxes each year thereafter? Would that have been a good decision? Yes!

We often meet people who wonder whether they are getting good advice from their current advisors. The answer is that it depends. Here are some questions to ask yourself to determine whether you are already doing proactive tax planning:

- Did you receive information from your advisor that helped to cut your tax bill?

- Do you meet with your tax advisor throughout the year as your business and investments take shape?

- Do you receive updates throughout the year on new tax changes or opportunities that arise?

If you answered yes to these questions, congratulations, you are among the 5% who actually do proactive tax planning. If you answered no to these questions, now is the best time to contact your tax advisor for a meeting.

Whom Should You Work With?

Most people see their CPA only once a year, during tax time. After that, they steer clear until it is time to do it all over again the following year. This, however, is not the relationship you want with your CPA. Your tax advisor should be an active member of your wealth-building team, not just the bearer of bad news come tax season. They should be someone you look forward to meeting, someone who will help you keep more money in your pocket rather than giving it to Uncle Sam. But you do need to be careful—just because you like your tax advisor does not necessarily mean they are the best tax advisor for you.

For example, if your father-in-law has a CPA practice that specializes in manufacturing businesses, he may not be the best person to do the taxes for your real estate business. Ever try to fire your father-in-law? We actually had a client, Tim, do just that. Even though he had been extremely afraid of having that conversation, Tim told us his father-in-law was actually relieved to learn he no longer had to do Tim's taxes, because it just was not his specialty.

What about your old buddy from college who works in accounting at Google? If he does not do taxes full-time and does not understand real estate, he is probably not the best person to help you. Just like there are specialties within the medical field, specialties exist in the accounting field. A cardiologist would go to a dentist for help with their teeth, and the chief financial officer of a large company would go to a tax advisor for tax assistance. In fact, we have quite a few clients who are practicing CPAs. Most of them come to us for help specifically with their real estate investments and strategies.

Changing tax advisors is not easy and not something you want to do very often. So if you are in the market for a new advisor, take the time to interview and find the best one you can afford. Ask for recommendations from fellow investors and meet with all the candidates. Make sure they understand you and your real estate business. Most importantly, make sure you trust and are comfortable working with them.

What Does All This Mean?

As a real estate investor, you have at your disposal a gigantic toolkit of strategies for minimizing your taxes each year. You just need to know how to apply those strategies. Saving taxes is more than simply minimizing your tax liabilities. It means more cash flow for you to enjoy, invest, and grow. Remember, it's not about how much money you make but how much money you keep. We wish you the best in your investing future!

Appendix A: Tax Freedom Day

According to TaxFoundation.Org, Tax Freedom Day is the day when the nation as a whole has earned enough money to pay its total taxes for the year. Tax Freedom Day is calculated by taking into consideration all federal, state, and local taxes and dividing them by the nation's total income. In 2015, Americans were expected to pay $3.28 trillion in federal taxes and $1.57 trillion in state and local taxes, for a total tax bill of $4.85 trillion, or 31% of the national income.

For illustrative purposes, we have chosen the year 2014 and created the following snapshot to better demonstrate these figures. How long exactly did Americans work to pay all federal, state, and local taxes for the 2014 calendar year? One hundred and ten days!

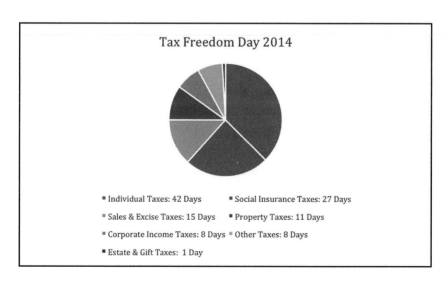

Tax Freedom Day 2014

- Individual Taxes: 42 Days
- Social Insurance Taxes: 27 Days
- Sales & Excise Taxes: 15 Days
- Property Taxes: 11 Days
- Corporate Income Taxes: 8 Days
- Other Taxes: 8 Days
- Estate & Gift Taxes: 1 Day

Appendix B: Glossary

Do you ever feel like CPAs and attorneys have their own language? They do! The better you can understand this "secret language," the better results you will have. To help you, we have put together this accounting glossary with some of the most commonly used terms in the real estate and financial world.

Please note that these are not official Webster's dictionary definitions, just our simplified explanations to help you understand these regularly used financial and real estate terms.

Accelerated depreciation

Depreciation taken in excess of the straight-line method.

Account

A section in a ledger devoted to a single aspect of a business (bank accounts, rent expense account).

Accounting

Refers to the overall process of tracking a business's income and expenses, and then using these numbers in various calculations and formulas to answer specific questions about the financial and tax status of the business.

Accounting equation

Represents both the relationship among a business's assets, liabilities, and equity and the double-entry system of financial statement presentation: A = Assets, L = Liabilities, O/E = Owner's Equity Assets = Liability + Equity

Accounting period

Time period an account report covers.

Accounts payable

Amount due, but not yet paid, by a business.

Accounts receivable

Amount due to, but not yet received by, a business.

Accruals (or accrued expenses)

Expenses that have been incurred by a business, but no invoice has been received. Typical accrued expense items are accrued interest or accrued property taxes.

Accrual method of accounting

A method in which accounts payable and accrued expenses are recorded so that the resulting expense reduces the income, and accounts receivable are recorded so that the unpaid, but due, receipt is counted as income.

Accrued expenses

Expenses incurred during an accounting period for which payment is postponed.

Accrued income

Income from revenues earned but not yet received.

Accrued interest

Interest incurred but not paid since the previous due date.

Accrued liability

Liabilities that are incurred, but for which payment is not yet made.

Accumulated depreciation account

A balance sheet account that holds the depreciation of a fixed asset until the end of the asset's useful life. It is credited each year with that year's depreciation.

ACRS (Accelerated Cost Recovery System)

A system of depreciation authorized by the U.S. Congress for tax purposes. Rapid write-off of the cost of assets.

Ad valorem (according to value)

Taxes are either ad valorem or specific. A tax of $5 per $1,000 of value is ad valorem, whereas a tax of $5 per house is specific.

Adjustable-rate mortgage (ARM)

The interest rate of a mortgage that varies based on conditions spelled out in the original terms of the mortgage.

Adjusted basis

Used to determine depreciation and gain or loss on the disposition of an asset. The adjusted basis in an asset is the beginning basis, decreased by depreciation, depletion, or any Section 179 deduction taken or increased by capital additions.

Adjusted gross income (AGI)

Annualized total income, at the bottom of the first page of the U.S. Individual Income Tax Return Form 1040, before exclusions and deductions.

Adjusting journal entries (AJE)

Accounting entries that are made to correct or record activities to one's financial statements.

ADR (the Class Life Asset Depreciation Range System)

A flexible set of government guidelines for depreciation that establishes an "asset depreciation period" rather than using the useful life.

AICPA

American Institute of Certified Public Accountants.

Amortization

The gradual reduction of an amount by means of equal periodic payments. This could include amortization of debt, where the periodic payments of principal and interest reduce the debt. The term amortization can also describe the spreading of an intangible item over its expected useful life. The amortization is similar to depreciation in this second definition.

Annualize

To convert anything into a yearly figure. For example, if profit is $1,000 per month, the annualized profit would be $12,000.

Appreciation

Increase in the value of an asset in excess of its depreciable cost, which is due to economic and other conditions, as distinguished from increases in value due to improvements or additions made to the asset.

Arm's length transaction

A transaction that is conducted as though the parties were unrelated, thereby avoiding any semblance of conflict of interest.

Assets

A balance sheet that shows what a business owns or is due, including bank accounts, equipment, vehicles, and buildings. Typical breakdown would include fixed assets, current assets, and noncurrent assets. Fixed assets are equipment, buildings, and vehicles.

Assumable mortgage

The mortgage on a property that can be assumed by another party at the time of purchase without that party having to qualify.

At-risk rule

An IRS rule that limits the amount of losses that may be deducted in any tax year from business activities to the amount of cash and the adjusted basis of other property contributed by the taxpayer.

Audit

Inspection of the accounting records and procedures of a business, government unit, or other reporting entity by a trained accountant for the purpose of verifying the accuracy and completeness of the records. May be conducted by a member of the organization (internal audit) or by an outsider (independent audit).

Audit trail

A list of transactions in the order in which they occurred.

Bad debts account

An account used with the accrual method of accounting. An income statement account that shows the write-off of unrecoverable debts from customers.

Balance sheet

A summary of the assets, liabilities, and equity accounts of a business. It typically reflects the historic cost of items (not their current value) as of a specific point in time.

Balloon payment

A repayment of the outstanding principal sum made at the end of a loan period.

Bank reconciliation

Verification of a bank statement balance and the depositor's checkbook balance.

Basis

Used in determining depreciation or gain or loss on the sale of property. In the simplest situation, the basis in property is the cost. It would also include the costs of any improvements capitalized.

Beneficiary

A person who derives advantage from something, especially a trust, will, or life insurance policy.

Bookkeeping

The activity or occupation of keeping records of the financial affairs of a business.

Book value

The value of a property as a capital asset (cost plus additions to value, less depreciation).

Boot

Describes property exchanged in a like-kind Section 1031 exchange that is not the property. An example of boot is the cash received in an exchange.

Business entity

Selection of the legal form under which a business is to operate: general partnership, C corporation, S corporation, limited partnership, or limited liability company are some examples. (Note that a sole proprietorship is generally not a legal business entity.)

Capital

An amount of money, goods, or services that have been contributed to a company in exchange for ownership.

Capital account

Term usually applied to an owner's equity in a business.

Capital asset

Assets of a permanent nature used to produce income, such as machinery, buildings, equipment, and land.

Capital gains

When a fixed asset is sold at a value more than the depreciable basis (original asset minus accumulated depreciation), the difference is often referred to as capital gains. These gains are either short term (assets had been held less than one year) or long term (asset had been held for more than a year).

Capitalization

Adding costs, such as improvements, to the basis of assets. This cost is then depreciated or amortized over time.

Cash and equivalents

All cash, marketplace securities, and other liquid items.

Cash basis/method of accounting

A method of accounting in which revenue and expenses are recorded in the period during which they are actually received or expended.

Cash flow

The flow of money in and out of a project or business over a period of time.

Cash flow financing

A form of financing in which the loan is backed by a company's expected cash flows.

Cash flow from investing

Money made or spent on long-term assets a company has purchased or sold.

Cash from operations

Money generated by a company's core business activities.

Cash-on-cash return

A ratio calculated by dividing the annual net cash received by the total cash invested in a project.

Certified financial statements

Financial statements that have undergone a formal audit by a certified public accountant.

Chart of accounts

A list of all the accounts.

Collateral substitution

The substitution of the underlying asset securing a debt.

Common stock

The most frequently issued class of stock. It usually provides a voting right but is secondary to preferred stock in dividend and liquidation rights.

Contra account

An account created to offset another account. An example would be accumulated depreciation offsetting the equipment account.

Cook the books

To falsify a set of accounts.

Corporation

Type of business organization chartered by a state and given legal rights as a separate entity.

Credit

As used in double-entry bookkeeping, a credit will decrease assets, increase income, decrease expenses, or increase liabilities.

Creditors

Entities to which a debt is owed by another entity.

Current assets

Those assets of a company that are reasonably expected to be sold, realized in cash, or consumed during the normal operating cycle of the business (usually one year). Such assets include cash, accounts receivable, and money due usually within one year; short-term investments; government bonds; inventories; and prepaid expenses.

Current liabilities

Liabilities to be paid within one year of the balance sheet date. Such liabilities include accounts payable, taxes payable, and rent payable.

Dealer

Someone who buys and sells real estate as a business rather than holding property for rental operations or for long-term appreciation.

Debit

As used in bookkeeping, a debit increases an asset or expense. It records a reduction from revenue, net worth, or a liability account.

Deferred maintenance

Maintenance that is needed, but has not been performed, on a property for a period of time.

Depreciation

Amount of expense charged against an asset by a company to write off the cost of the asset over its useful life.

Due on sale clause

A clause present in most mortgages that permits the lenders to declare the full balance of the loan due and payable upon the sale or transfer of ownership of a property.

Earned income

Income earned by an individual or within a trade or business. Depending on the business structure, the net earned income may be subject to self-employment tax in addition to regular income tax.

Equity

The value of a business in excess of all liabilities against the business.

Expense

Cost incurred in the normal course of business to generate revenue.

Fair market value

The highest price offered in a competitive market. Determined by negotiation between an informed, willing, and capable buyer and an informed, willing, and capable seller.

Financial statement

An accounting statement showing the assets and liabilities of a person or company.

Fixed assets

Assets that are purchased for long-term use and are not likely to be converted quickly into cash. Examples include land, buildings, and equipment.

Fixed assets (net)

All fixed assets net of accumulated depreciation taken previously.

Fix-up expenses (a.k.a. make-ready expenses)

Maintenance and repair costs incurred to rehabilitate a property to get it ready for sale or rent.

Flip property

A property that is purchased to be immediately resold for a profit. These properties may or may not require refurbishment.

Foreclosure

A proceeding in or out of court, to extinguish all rights, title, and interest of the owner(s) of property to sell the property to satisfy a lien against it.

Foreclosure sale

A sale of property used as security for a debt to satisfy said debt.

G&A expenses (general and administrative expenses)

Refers to the indirect overhead costs that are not necessarily associated with a specific property.

General ledger

Accounting records that show all the financial statement accounts of a business.

General partnership

Two or more partners who are jointly and severally responsible for the debts of the partnership. The partnership income is taxed at the individual partner's personal tax rate.

Gross income

The total amount of income received. Also see gross profit.

Gross profit

Refers to the gross income less the costs related to the item(s) sold.

Hard money

A specific type of financing through which a borrower receives funds. Private investors or companies typically issue hard money loans. Interest rates are generally higher than those for conventional commercial or residential property loans because of the loan's higher risk and shorter duration.

Impound account

An account in which the mortgage holder collects, in advance, an amount for the property tax and insurance on a periodic basis. When due, the expenses for these items are then paid from this account on the buyer's behalf.

Installment sale

Created when a property or asset is sold and the sales price is received over a series of payments, rather than all at once at the close of the sale.

Investor

A person who purchases property with the intention of retaining that property for investment purposes.

Joint return

U.S. federal income tax filing status that can be used by a married couple. The married couple must be married as of the last day of the tax year to qualify for this filing status.

K-1

The information form received from a partnership, S corporation, trust, or estate tax return, which provides the flow-through income and losses to be reported on an investor's individual return.

Land trust

A revocable trust that is sometimes used to transfer ownership without public notice.

Lease

An agreement by which an owner of real property (lessor) gives the right of possession to another (lessee) for a specified period of time (term) and for a specified consideration (rent).

Lease option

Also known as lease with option to purchase. A lease under which the lessee has the right to purchase the property. The price and terms of the purchase must be set forth for the option to be valid.

Lessee

The tenant.

Lessor

The landlord.

Liability

A claim on the assets of an entity that must be paid or otherwise honored by that entity.

Like kind

Refers to property that is similar to another for which it has been exchanged. The definitions of like kind properties can be found in the United States tax code at Section 1031 and the related regulations, revenue rulings, revenue procedures, and case law.

Listing

A contract between a licensed agent and a principal giving authorization to the agent to market the principal's property.

Loan-to-value

The ratio of the loan amount divided by the total value of the property.

Long-term debt

Debt that is due to be paid after one year, including bonds, debentures, bank debt, mortgages, and capital lease obligations.

Mortgagee

A lender who loans money to a mortgagor. Real estate or other assets usually secure the loan.

Mortgagor

Receiver of the proceeds of a mortgage who is then responsible for the payments.

Negative amortization

A negatively amortizing loan is one in which the payments do not cover the interest portion of the loan balance. The loan increases in amount as time goes on.

Net income (a.k.a net profit)

Difference between total revenue and total expenses.

Net operating loss (NOL)

The loss experienced by a business or individual when business deductions exceed business income for the fiscal year.

Nexus

Taxpayer's base of operations for state income tax purposes.

Non-recourse financing

Financing that does not require the personal guarantees of owners or others. The collateral is sufficient to secure the loan.

Option

A right to buy an asset, such as property, that is granted by the owner of the asset named in the option agreement. The option holder has the right but not the obligation to purchase.

Organizational costs

Amounts spent to begin a business entity, including filing fees, franchise acquisition, and legal fees.

Phantom income

Taxable income where no cash is received from the transaction.

Points

Additional fees paid to a lender. Points are generally stated as a percentage of the total amount paid by the person who borrowed the money.

Portfolio income

Income that is earned by money invested—typically, interest, dividends, and capital gains.

Pre-foreclosure

Time period during which the homeowner is in default but before the actual foreclosure action when they lose their ownership in the home.

Preferred stock

Nonvoting (typically) capital stock that pays dividends at a specified rate and has preference over common stock in the payment of dividends and the liquidation of assets.

Prepaid expenses

Amounts that are paid in advance to a vender or creditor for goods and services.

Principal residence (a.k.a personal residence)

An IRS designation for a taxpayer's primary home.

Property tax

Generally, a tax levied by the county on both real and personal property. The amount of the tax is dependent on the value of the property.

Real estate activities

A list of activities defined by the IRS that qualify for calculation of Real Estate Professional Status.

Real estate dealer

As determined by the IRS based on fifteen factors. Primarily used for real estate owners who buy property to sell it for profit. The IRS treats this as a business, and the income from the sale is considered earned income.

Real estate developer

As determined by the IRS, a taxpayer who buys land or properties to build and then sell.

Real estate professional

As determined by the IRS, an individual who has met the hours-worked criteria for real estate activities.

Realized income

The amount of gain that is earned but that may or may not be taxable, depending on exceptions in the tax law.

Recapture

The portion of a depreciation taken in excess of straight-line rates that has previously escaped taxation and is returned, or recaptured, when the property is sold.

Recognized income

The portion of gain on the disposition of an asset that is taxable.

Rent-to-own

A form of lease option in which a sale does not occur until the tenant/future buyer purchases the property.

Reverse mortgage

A type of loan that increases in balance as the owner draws against it. Typically used with older homeowners looking for a way to tap into their equity.

Reversing entry

A debit or credit bookkeeping entry made to reverse a prior bookkeeping entry.

Short-term asset

An asset expected to be converted into cash within the normal operating cycle (usually one year or less).

Short-term liability

A liability that will come due in one year or less.

Sole proprietor

An individual who owns a business. A sole proprietor has unlimited liability for business debts and obligations. This is also known as a Schedule C business.

Sole proprietorship

A form of business organization that has only one owner and an unincorporated status.

Stepped-up basis

The new basis in an asset that is greater than the asset's prior basis. This can occur when a new owner inherits property from a decedent.

Straight-line depreciation

Depreciation expense computed at an equal annual rate so that the cost (or other basis) will be expensed over its useful life.

Tax bracket

The highest percentage of income tax that you pay, based on graduated tax tables.

Tax credit

Directly reduces the amount of tax you pay.

Tax deduction

Reduces your taxable income.

Tax deferred

Taxes will be deferred to a later time but not eliminated.

Tax free

No taxes will ever be assessed.

Total assets

Total of all assets, both current and fixed.

Total current assets

Total of cash and equivalents, trade receivables, inventory, and all other existing assets.

Total current liabilities

Total of short term notes payable, current maturities of Long Term Debt, trade payable, income taxes payable, and all other current liabilities.

Unrealized income

Profit that has been made but not yet realized or collected through a transaction.

Wrap-around mortgage

A new mortgage loan, subordinate to and encompassing an existing mortgage loan.

Acknowledgments

We would like to express our deepest gratitude to the many people who made this book possible.

First and foremost is the wonderful family that surrounds us. Thank you to our amazing parents and grandparents who have supported and inspired us since we were born. To our extended family and friends, thank you for the love you have provided us during every step of our journey. To our loyal puppies, Daisy and Bruin, who are our constant cheerleaders, your enthusiasm and love is endless and contagious. Finally, to our amazing four-year-old son, Austin, you have shown us a love we never knew was possible.

Thank you to all of our team members at Keystone CPA, Inc. who helped us to develop the strategies in this book, as well as to share these with our clients. Your daily commitment to servicing the firm and its clients, with dedication and passion, has made this book possible. A special thank you to Courtney Chambers, who spent countless hours to help us bring the amazing tax stories to life with her skillful writing abilities.

Thank you to our colleagues and mentors over the years for challenging us to be the best advisors that we can be. Your experience, knowledge, and guidance have enabled us to build a firm that we are very proud of.

Thank you as well to all of our hundreds of clients over the years that have put your trust in us. You have taught us at least as much as we taught you, and this book would not have been possible without your input and ideas.

Finally, a special thank you to Josh Dorkin, Brandon Turner, Kimberly Peticolas, and the entire community at BiggerPockets.com. You took a chance to invite us for what you thought might be a "boring" tax podcast and two years later we are grateful to be working with you on our first book dedicated to helping real estate investors everywhere.

To all of these people we are deeply grateful.

MORE FROM BIGGERPOCKETS

If you enjoyed this book, we hope you'll take a moment to check out some of the other great material BiggerPockets offers. BiggerPockets.com is the real estate investing social network, marketplace, and information hub, designed to help make you a smarter real estate investor through podcasts, blog posts, videos, forums, files, and more.

First and foremost, BiggerPockets is a **social network**. This means no matter where you go on the site, you can engage with others and grow your knowledge, skills, and confidence.

The BiggerPockets **Forums** are designed to give you a platform to ask or answer questions involving real estate. With hundreds of conversations happening all the time—and 1,962,721 forum posts, there is a topic for everyone.

The BiggerPockets **Blog** is the most influential real estate investing blog in the world today. With in-depth topics ranging from landlording, house flipping, note investing, wholesaling, and more discussed every day, you'll never run out of topics to read about.

The BiggerPockets **Marketplace** is THE go-to destination on Bigger-Pockets if you are looking to buy or sell a property, get financing, advertise your business, or look for partners. The Marketplace is the central location where business is done on BiggerPockets.

You can learn even more about real estate investing by reading our other great books from BiggerPockets Publishing.

Sign up today—it's **free!** www.BiggerPockets.com

The Book on Rental Property Investing

by Brandon Turner

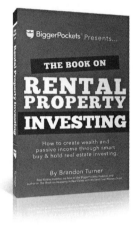

In *The Book on Rental Property Investing*, real estate investor and co-host of the Bigger-Pockets Podcast Brandon Turner has one goal in mind: to give you every strategy, tool, tip, and technique needed to become a millionaire rental property investor—while helping you avoid the junk that pulls down so many wannabies!

Written for both new and experienced investors, this book will impart years of experience through the informative and entertaining lessons contained within. You'll find practical, up-to-date, exciting strategies that investors across the world are using to build wealth and significant cash flow through rental properties.

This book will show you:

- Why many real estate investors fail, and how you can ensure you don't!
- 4 unique, easy-to-follow strategies you can begin implementing today.
- Creative tips for finding incredible deals—even in hot, competitive markets.
- How to achieve success without touching a toilet, paint or broom.
- Actionable ideas for financing rentals, no matter how much cash you have.
- Practical advice on keeping your wealth by deferring (and eliminating) taxes.
- And so much more!

The Book on Managing Rental Properties

By Brandon and Heather Turner

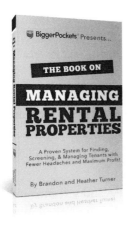

No matter how great you are at finding good rental property deals, you could lose everything if you don't manage your properties correctly! But being a landlord doesn't have to mean middle-of-the-night phone calls, costly evictions, or daily frustrations with ungrateful tenants. Being a landlord can actually be fun IF you do it right.

That's why Brandon and Heather Turner put together this comprehensive book that will change the way you think of being a landlord forever. Written with both new and experienced landlords in mind, The Book on Managing Rental Properties takes you on an insider tour of the Turners' management business, so you can discover exactly how they've been able to maximize their profit, minimize their stress, and have a blast doing it!

This book will teach you:

- The suble mindset shift that will increase your chance at success 100x!
- Low-cost strategies for attracting the best tenants who won't rip you off.
- 7 tenant types we'll NEVER rent to—and that you shouldn't either!
- 19 provisions that your rental lease should have to protect YOU.
- Practical tips on training your tenant to pay on time and stay long term.
- How to take the pain and stress out of your bookkeeping and taxes.
- And so much more!

The Book on Investing in Real Estate with No (and Low) Money Down

By Brandon Turner

In The Book on Investing in Real Estate with No (and Low) Money Down, active real estate investor (and co-host of the world famous BiggerPockets Podcast), Brandon Turner takes readers past the hype and dives into multiple real life strategies that investors across the world are using to invest in real estate using creativity rather than their own cash.

Written for both new and seasoned investors alike, this book will walk you through numerous strategies for financing a variety of investment properties.

In this book, you'll discover:

- Where to find low down payment bank loans
- How to get your first property despite a lack of experience and cash
- The good, bad, and ugly side of partnerships
- The best ways to raise private money from others
- Strategies for finding and using hard money loans
- How to wholesale your way to success
- and so much more!

The Book on Flipping Houses
By J. Scott

The Book on Flipping Houses, written by active real estate fix-and-flipper J Scott, contains more than 300 pages of detailed, step-by-step training perfect for both the complete newbie and the seasoned pro looking to build a killer house-flipping business.

Whatever your skill level, *The Book on Flipping Houses* will teach you everything you need to know to build a profitable, efficient house-flipping business and start living the life of your dreams.

Get it at www.biggerpockets.com/flippingbook

The Book on Estimating Rehab Costs
By J. Scott

One of the most difficult tasks for a real estate investor is estimating repairs. To help you overcome this obstacle, J Scott and BiggerPockets pull back the curtain on the rehab process and show you not only the cost ranges and details associated with each and every aspect of a rehab, but also the framework and methodology for estimating rehab costs. You'll discover how to accurately estimate the variety of costs you will likely face while rehabbing a home as well as which upgrade options offer the biggest bang for your buck.

Whether you are an experienced home renovation specialist or still learning how to screw in a light bulb, this valuable resource will be your guide to staying on budget, managing contractor pricing, and ensuring a timely profit.

Get it at www.biggerpockets.com/rehabbook.

FREE Ebook: *The Ultimate Beginner's Guide to Real Estate Investing*
By Joshua Dorkin and Brandon Turner

The Ultimate Beginner's Guide to Real Estate Investing is a free guide designed to help you build a solid foundation for your venture into real estate. In the eight chapters of this book, you'll learn how to best gain an education (for free), how to pick a real estate niche, and how to find, fund, and manage your latest real estate investment.

Get it free today at www.biggerpockets.com/ubg.